List & S.B. No.	Name	Rating	Port Division and Official No.	Whence Entered	Date	Whither Discharged	Date

H.M.S. Amethyst

B C D E F G H I J K L M N O P S

L st & S.B. No.	Name	Rating	Port Division and Official No.	Whence Entered	Date	Whither Discharged	Date

List & S.B. No.	Name	Rating	Port Division and Official No.	Whence Entered	Date	Whither Discharged	Date

Tuesday 19TH April 1949.

0800 Slipped from Holts Wharf, Shanghai & sailed for Nanking.

1832 Exchanged identies with Yet Sen, Chinese Destroyer, Senior Officer of that section of the Yangtse. Anchored at Kuang Yin.
Ship was advised to darken by Chinese S.O. This was agreed to. The ship was therefore darkened at Sunset, with yardarm groups rigged to illuminate the Union Jacks on the Ship's side at short notice.
Chinese vessels anchored at Kuang Yin :-
   1 Sloop. YET SEN. Senior Officer.
   1 Escort vessel of Jap. origin.
   2 L.C.T. (L)'s. Which moved during the night.
   1 L.C.T Which was unloading stores?
The night was uneventful, though a few signal flares were reported.

Wednesday 20th April.

0515 Ship weighed anchor and proceeded up river to Nanking from Kuang Yin. The ship assumed a three watch cruising organisation.

0630 Owing to bad visibility due to fog the ship anchored until such times as it improved.

0730 Visibility improved, ship weighed anchor and proceeded up river at 8 knots.

0800 Hands to action stations, a warning had been given that this would be done 10 minutes earlier.

0832 The ship was fired on from the North bank.
An order was given to the Director to get on the bearing from which the fire was coming, this was initially small arms fire

L st & S.B. No.	Name	Rating	Port Division and Official No.	Whence Entered	Date	Whither Discharged	Date

List & S.B. No.	Name	Rating	Port Division and Official No.	Whence Entered	Date	Whither Discharged	Date

20th Cont.

but later developed into light Artillery.
The ship increased speed to 15 knots.
The director was never able to identify the
target and did not at any time report ON.
An attempt was made to open fire with the
Orlikons but was cancelled by the check
fire bell before a round had been fired.
A broadcast was made to X guns crew over
the action broadcast system to unfurl the
Union Jacks in position, but furled on
the ships side. This was done.

0845 Firing ceased, Amethyst was not hit, had
not opened fire and proceeded up river.

0915 Firing was reopened on the ship whilst
in the Kou An Road, off the North end of
Tai Ping Chow. Several direct hits were
registered, the first killing one rating
and seriously wounding the coxswain who
was on the wheel, in the wheelhouse,
leaving one Leading Seaman (L/SEA L. FRANK)
in the wheelhouse. This rating was also
hit in the back and was out for a few
seconds, when he came round, he
immediately took over the wheel and reported
to the bridge. Full speed ahead was
ordered from the bridge and rung on from
the wheelhouse. Whilst the ship was
going at full speed the Gyro warning
light came on and then the gyro repeat
light went off. FRANK reported to the
bridge that the Gyro had gone off, also
his magnetic course which he continued
to steer, although getting no reply from
the bridge, the reason for no reply apparently
was that another shell had hit the

L st & S.B. No.	Name	Rating	Port Division and Official No.	Whence Entered	Date	Whither Discharged	Date

List & S.B. No.	Name	Rating	Port Division and Official No.	Whence Entered	Date	Whither Discharged	Date

20th CONT.

bridge, wounding the Captain, Navigator, 1st Lieut, Action Officer of the Watch, the Asdic operator and killing the communication number. The G.C.O. was ordered by the Captain to engage the ~~target~~ target and passed the necessary orders, to the T.S.

A second shot landed in the vicinity of the bridge and FULL ASTERN together was ordered (by the 1st Lieut. who had come round and got to the voice pipe) A.B. FRANK repeated the order and rang on the Port telegraph to full astern, then found that the Star. telegraph had jammed in the full F.HEAD position and could not be moved, FRANK reported to the bridge but could get no reply, then tried to reach the engine room by voice pipe, but could get no reply from there, (inspection afterwards showed that the voicepipe had been broken in half, along the Star passage) FRANK rung down Stop on the Port telegraph, the ship in the meantime having swung towards the South Bank, the reports that A & B guns will not bear were received. in the director and the order to SHOOT was passed to X gun but this having no effect the G.C.O. ordered X gun to open fire in local control on the armament broadcast, after a short delay X Gun opened fire. This delay was caused by a direct hit wrecking the low power switch—board. Neither the Bofor or Orlikons opened fire. By this time the ship was aground on the Eastern Bank of LO CHENG CHOW (Rose Island) The ship was now lying stern on to the enemy battery, sited at San Chiang Yin, with the Port side

L st & S.B. No.	Name	Rating	Port Division and Official No.	Whence Entered	Date	Whither Discharged	Date

List & S.B. No.	Name	Rating	Port Division and Official No.	Whence Entered	Date	Whither Discharged	Date

20th Cont.

slightly exposed. Throughout the ship was under
fire continuously and received about 42 direct
hits. One shot was a direct hit on the
right gun of X, killing and wounding all
the right guns crew, also two of the left
crew. Fire broke out which proved to be
burning cordite, which was extinguished by
Pyrene & Foamite.

At this stage the Captain was unconscious
and the 1st Lieutenant (Lt G.L. Weston D.S.C.) although
badly wounded assumed Command.

All the wounded were taken down below,
most of them to the After Mess deck to receive
treatment.

Bren guns and small arms were mustered and
fire opened with these.

At the same time the 1st Lieutenant ordered
all boats to be lowered in which to send
the wounded ashore, the Starboard whaler being
the only undamaged boat, was lowered whilst
attempts were made to repair the motor boat,
this was unsuccessful as a direct hit on the
stern wrecked it completely, killing two and
wounding others. The Carley rafts were then
slipped.

The ship was still under heavy fire and a
hit on the quarter deck where the wounded
were being collected ready to send ashore, killed
the Doctor (Surg Lt. Alderton) & his Sick Berth Attendant
(S.B.A Baker) and also killed several of the
wounded.

As the casualties still continued to mount it
was decided to abandon the ship.

A volunteer party to man the whaler and
evacuate the wounded was called for and obtained.

L st & S.B. No.	Name	Rating	Port Division and Official No.	Whence Entered	Date	Whither Discharged	Date

About sixty ratings swam ashore, but were fired upon in the water both by small arms and artillery, and no one else was allowed to leave the ship.

A WHITE flag was hoisted at the yard arm in order to prevent further casualties and to attempt to parley with the Communist leaders and explain to them that the ship was British. The firing continued for some time after this but eventually it stopped.

At the same time any movement on deck or attempts to assist the wounded on X gun deck or the quarter deck immediately produced small arms fire from the North Bank. In spite of this, the wounded were got under cover. Also inspite of the small arms fire the G.I P.O. H. Freeman & 4/Sea. L. FRANK ran a wire from the Starboard after reel along the Quarter Deck and out through the after fair lead in case that when the "Consort" comes down from Nanking she will try to tow us off the mud, later this proved to be impossible, if not quiet that, it was absolutely out of the question.

Of those that swam ashore it was later learnt that about 50 of them reached Shanghai, about 10 remained on the bank and later returned to the ship, one was killed (Cʰ Sᵗᵒ. AUBREY), and three were carried down river and picked up by Consort, one is missing and two were taken to hospital ashore.

Casualties   Killed   1 officer (Nᵒ) & 16 Ratings
                        1 Rating Ch Sto known drowned.

              Wounded 5 Officers (including Captain) & 20 ratings.

All C.B & S.P's were collected to transfer to Consort, burnt or sunk as the situation might demand. All Toᵖ Secret publications were destroyed.

L st & S.B. No.	Name	Rating	Port Division and Official No.	Whence Entered	Date	Whither Discharged	Date

20TH CONT.

Emergency power from Main L.P. batteries was provided for T.C.S. set, aldis lamp (B Gun deck) and lighting in the After Mess deck.

Main Lower Power batteries not hit but discharged partially through L.P switchboard being wrecked by 105 mm shell – one of the first to hit the ship.

At about 1400 Consort was sighted and eventually Visual signalling range was reduced. Amethyst advised Consort to go back as she might find herself in our position, and asked her to set watch on a T.C.S. frequency. W/T communication was never established. Consort continued down river under heavy fire, and returning the fire she signalled, "Is it possible to tow you off". Amethyst replied only if the battery is silenced first. Consort then continued down river turned about and returned firing all guns at the North Bank. She turned again of TEIN FU CHOW and continued down river.

Nationalist Soldiers appeared on Rose Island and shouted at the ship, the whaler was sent inshore with the gunner in charge. He went to the Nationalist head-quarters and was told that our casualties could be evacuated by the Nationalists if sent ashore. This was not acceptable at the time as it was still considered possible to refloat the ship and proceed to Nanking by night, under cover of darkness.

The party then returned to the ship including 10 of the party who had swam ashore in the forenoon.

No fire had been experienced since about 1500.

1930 Steam was raised again in Both boilers.

2245. Slow – Half & Full speed astern, wheel hard

L st & S.B. No.	Name	Rating	Port Division and Official No.	Whence Entered	Date	Whither Discharged	Date

List & S.B. No.	Name	Rating	Port Division and Official No.	Whence Entered	Date	Whither Discharged	Date

20ᵀᴴ CONT.

Starboard – Hard Port etc etc were rung on and orders passed and everything possible was done to free the ship off the mud.

2330 Orders were given to lighten the ship forward, by jettisoning, heavy weights forward, single derrick, awning stanchions and by pumping out oil fuel from Noˢ 1 & 2 tanks.

Thursday 21ˢᵗ April

0010 A second attempt was made to free the ship.

0015 Full astern both, Ship afloat, proceed up river.

0045 Ship under small arms fire off FU TE WEI.

0130 Ship retired and anchored off TA HSEN WE for the night. No further fire experienced.

0800 Hands to muster on quarter deck, mustered all wounded & killed.

1000 Chinese Nationalist Army officer arrived onboard to discuss medical aid

1030 Two more officers arrive, they agreed to provide sampans to transfer wounded to Sunderland A/c.

1130 Weighed in accordance with signal from "London" that she was coming up river to escort Amethyst down river, owing to heavy opposition London was unable to reach Amethyst.

1150 Amethyst returned to original anchorage, ship was not fired upon.

1530 Chinese doctor and two medical orderlies arrive by sampan.

1630 Sunderland flying boat with medical supplies and two doctors (one R.N & one R.A.F) circled the ship and landed; R.A.F. doctor landed. Battery at San Chiang Yin opened fire, flying boat took off. Ship weighed and proceeded up river, and anchored under fire at HSIAO HO CREEK. Gunner stranded on aircraft.

L st & S.B. No.	Name	Rating	Port Division and Official No.	Whence Entered	Date	Whither Discharged	Date

List & S.B. No.	Name	Rating	Port Division and Official No.	Whence Entered	Date	Whither Discharged	Date

21ST CONT

1830 — Chinese doctor went ashore to arrange for the evacuation of the wounded.

2000 — 12 Sampans approach the ship, all wounded evacuated except minor injuries and Lt. G.L. Weston. Total landed 20; of these the Captain Lt. Com. B.M. Skinner & Able-seaman Winter later died of wounds.

2330 — Evacuation of wounded completed.

Friday 22nd April.

0100 — Ship weighed anchor and proceeded up river about 10 miles.

0230 — Anchored again, position based on directions received. Small arms firing at ship, started from South Bank as soon as the anchor was dropped - Jack on ships side illuminated, but firing continued.

0235 — Weighed and proceeded about 1 mile down stream and anchored off Chen Pi Chen Mou.

0800 — Hands fall in, muster for cleaning ship and preparing the dead for burial.

1315 — Sunderland circled the ship and endeavoured unsuccessfully to establish visual signal communications. Fire was opened on the aircraft when she attempted to land by the battery, situated at Pu Shun Wei area, aircraft once again took to her wings, whilst Amethyst weighed anchor and proceeded up river and anchored about 6 cables N.N.E off TAN TA CHEN.

Landing craft approached the ship from up river and came alongside, onboard was Lt. Com. J.S. Kerans. R.N. A.N.A at Nanking, who had come down to take Command of the ship in place of Lt. G.L. Weston D.S.C. who went ashore for Nanking &

L st & S.B. No.	Name	Rating	Port Division and Official No.	Whence Entered	Date	Whither Discharged	Date

List & S.B. No.	Name	Rating	Port Division and Official No.	Whence Entered	Date	Whither Discharged	Date
	Hospital for an operation for removal of shrapnel from his lung.						
1630	17 Dead buried, with full Naval Honours except for the salute.						
	Night intention – to proceed to Nanking – later abandoned, on instructions from H.K. Prepared to destroy ship.						
2200	Six Chinese Nationalist war ship proceeding down river.						

Saturday 23rd April.

0800	Uneventful night. Hands to muster and rig splinter protection, round "B" Gun — Bridge – Wheelhouse and W/T office. Repair as much damage as possible. Night intention to proceed down river.						
1200	Activity on TA SHA about 2 miles away to N.W. shifted berth down river, came under fire from PU SHEN WEI battery, turned up river and anchored off MA CHAN SHAR. THREE rounds fired at the ship, no hits received.						
1400	Communists crossing in strength in TAU MEN SHAN Area. Night intention to proceed down river abandoned in view of Communist crossings. Prepared to abandon ship if so compelled by fire from both beaches.						
2230	Units of the Chinese Navy proceeded down river and opened fire on North Bank, fire was returned, fires were started ashore.						
2315	Gun fire receding into the distance.						

Sunday 24th April.

0800	Making water in the wardroom, list on ship to starboard. Pumped out wardroom and repaired damage with cement. All unnecessary top weight jettisoned, Motor Boat–						

L st & S.B. No.	Name	Rating	Port Division and Official No.	Whence Entered	Date	Whither Discharged	Date

List & S.B. No.	Name	Rating	Port Division and Official No.	Whence Entered	Date	Whither Discharged	Date

24th CONT.

Kedge anchor — Awning stanchions — 293 Aerial & Pedestal
Fire risks reduced by jettisoning ready use
ammunition — Fireworks etc.

1000 — Ship now on even keel.

1100 — Civilian junk traffic appears to be reverting
to normal.

1145 — Church service on the after mess deck.

Monday 25th April.

Signs of Communist movement on both banks
of the river. Small junk traffic seems to
be nearly normal. All quiet.

0800 — Hands, Stopping leaks and generally making
the ship sea worthy, & diminishing fire risks.

1200 — Motor vessels passed with Communist troops
onboard, bugle blown at the ship to
attract attention.

1230 — Ship was hailed by three soldiers on the
South Bank, who signaled for some one
to go ashore, the chinese steward could
not understand their speech from this
range. They later retired.

1445 — The same three returned and one of them
held a letter, they renewed their efforts
to signify that some one should be sent
ashore.

1515 — The whaler was lowered and pulled ashore with
P.O. Freeman incharge. On arrival ashore he
had a friendly interview with the local
Artillery Commander, who had fired at and
damaged the ship.
Interview brought out the following points,
Chinese considered Amethyst opened fire first.
We should not be fired upon unless we moved
or caused trouble.

L st & S.B. No.	Name	Rating	Port Division and Official No.	Whence Entered	Date	Whither Discharged	Date

List & S.B. No.	Name	Rating	Port Division and Official No.	Whence Entered	Date	Whither Discharged	Date

He could give no answer about the missing ratings. He had suffered 250 casualties.

1930 | P.O. Freeman returned to the ship.

Whaler was hoisted on return.

Wednesday 27th April

1150 | Clear lower deck, hands muster on the Quarter Deck for photographs.

1200 | Junk approached ship with two soldiers onboard with letter from battery commander requesting an interview with the Captain.

Lt K.S. Hett went ashore in the junk to meet the battery commander Interview was cordial, but B.C. still insisted that Amethyst opened fire first. This was repeatedly and emphatically denied. A dead lock was reached on this point.

He stated that he could not give the ship a guaranteed passage down river but said it could be arranged by the Ambassador.

He said that Nationalist ships were still up river, and the batteries further down the river might fire on us although he himself would not.

He stated that the high casualties received by Peoples Liberation Army was due to concentration at San Chiang Yin waiting to cross the river.

He had no news of missing ratings but would try to find there whereabouts, in which case they could only return to the ship before it was allowed to proceed down river.

When asked he said that he would try and arrange a meeting between Lt Hett and the General in Chinkiang for the next morning, but said the General was very busy and

L st & S.B. No.	Name	Rating	Port Division and Official No.	Whence Entered	Date	Whither Discharged	Date

27th Cont.

communications would not be established until that evening. Asked if 1 officer & 4 or 5 ratings could come ashore to facilitate ship shore communication he later stated that the peasantry ashore were frightened by the presence of Amethyst. The meeting was then concluded and the Major offered any assistance that the ship might require for obtaining fresh food. Lt. Hett returned onboard at about 1500.

Thursday 28th April.

All quiet & uneventful night. usual junk traffic. No further communication from shore received.

Friday 29th April.

Very bad weather. Very little movement on the river.

Saturday 30th April

Weather slightly improved. Still very little river traffic. Troop movement along the South Bank going on all day, both on foot & by lorry.

Sunday 1st May.

Weather still bad. Some movement on the river today. Clocks advanced 1 hour. Church on the after messdeck. pipe down.

Monday 2nd May.

Weather now fine, very much improved. A great deal of traffic across and up the river. 1730 Sampan came to the ship with Communist Army Captain and two soldiers. Brought the compliments of C in C Nanking. Stated free passage may be given in a few days ??? Asked for written statement of ships position and that she would not

L st & S.B. No.	Name	Rating	Port Division and Official No.	Whence Entered	Date	Whither Discharged	Date

List & S.B. No.	Name	Rating	Port Division and Official No.	Whence Entered	Date	Whither Discharged	Date

2nd May Cont.

move without permission of C in C. this was given. Had no news of wounded.

3rd May. Tuesday.

0930 — Sampan brought 3 Communist soldiers out to the ship to take our Chinese ashore to buy food. Chinese returned at 1300 hours with eggs paid for with rice & flour. Two tugs proceeded up river flying large red flags full of military personal. There arrival caused the Communist guns crews to close up at the double. There appeared to be a gun in the stern covered over with canvas. A wheel only was visible, with the soldiers peering out from under the canvas. There were about 40 soldiers visible in the first tug. The second tug followed similarly laden in about 20 minutes.

Side party sampan established.

Wednesday 4th May.

One river steamer flying large red flag, steamed up river with a large barque secured alongside. The vessel was named TAI FUNG and there were about 100 soldiers onboard. Battery crews were observed to be closed up.

Two traders from the village ashore came off to bargain for vegetables.

1115 — Nationalist air craft fired at TAI FUNG, it did not appear to be damaged and carried on up river.

Thursday 5th May.

The civilian contractor, with a soldier came out to the ship in the side party sampan, but for no apparent reason was sent ashore again.

List & S.B. No.	Name	Rating	Port Division and Official No.	Whence Entered	Date	Whither Discharged	Date

List & S.B. No.	Name	Rating	Port Division and Official No.	Whence Entered	Date	Whither Discharged	Date

5th May Cont.

Lieut. Hett went ashore to hasten if possible safe conduct and information of the two wounded. Side party sampan returned with two contractors and 65 lb potatoes. The garrison Commander sent a message onboard by the contractors for 4 or 5 of our cantonese chinese to go ashore, No specific reason given. Two were sent ashore with instructions not to give away any information, but to act dumb. Chinese returned onboard without an interview, the cantonese speaking communist not being at the garrison. Chinese on returning onboard appeared to be very nervous.

Friday 6th May.

At yesterdays interview Lt Hett was told, that aide Memoir had been despatched to Nanking, the messenger had not yet returned from Nanking with safe passage. Coft also promised to telephone Nanking tonight. The interview was unsatisfactory in every way.
Convoy of at least 50 lorries moving along road Eastward.

Saturday 7th May.

Convoy of lorries passing along the road throughout the night.
Single aircraft carried out bombing runs on the village 1 mile ahead of the ship off the Port bow at 0900 and again at 1700. Machine gun fire only was directed at the aircraft.
3 cwt of potatoes and a small quantity of greens received from the shore.

L st & S.B. No.	Name	Rating	Port Division and Official No.	Whence Entered	Date	Whither Discharged	Date

List & S.B. No.	Name	Rating	Port Division and Official No.	Whence Entered	Date	Whither Discharged	Date

Sunday 8th May.

Local Communist Command Captain came off with invitation to all our Chinese onboard to lunch. Invitation virtually an order. 2 permitted to remain onboard. Safe conduct on Wednesday. Interview brief

Church on after mess deck. Lower deck cleared after church. Captain spoke to the ships company.

Aircraft carried out reconnaissance flight over south bank and flew inland from there. Motor launch passed close down starboard side of the ship with passengers or should I say spectators? then continued down river. Naval members of the crew or party apparently did not wish to be seen from the ship. Lt Hett took photographs of the surrounding country side from up the mast. Convoys appear to be moving again this evening.

Monday 9th May.

Convoys continued throughout the night.

1145 Launch arrived to take the 6 Chinese to luncheon party at Chiang Sha.

Aircraft circled Chingkiang, was fired at, but apparently was only on a reconnaissance flight. "Control of movements," opened fire on a Tug with 4 junks in tow, Amethyst was foul of line of fire and small arm bullets passed over ship, endangering personnel onboard. Chinese returned onboard. Capt Tai Ko Lou was informed of the shooting, and a protest was made to him by the Captain of Amethyst. Chinese attended a luncheon party followed by a sight seeing tour, which was non-political according to But Sai Tin, Captains' steward and

L st & S.B. No.	Name	Rating	Port Division and Official No.	Whence Entered	Date	Whither Discharged	Date

List & S.B. No.	Name	Rating	Port Division and Official No.	Whence Entered	Date	Whither Discharged	Date

May 9th Cont.

intrepretor, there were no speeches or suggestions made.

Tuesday 10th May.

Uneventful day, nothing of note occured, everything quiet.

Wednesday 11th May.

To-day we had an occasional burst of machine gun firing on the South Bank, it seems probable that a practice range is sited there, although the firing is not frequent enough to fully substantiate this. Local garrison appeared to be employed laying cable, presumable that they are opening up a line telephony network.

In the evening motor craft & most of the Military craft moving on the river disappear down the creek at Chen Pi Chen Kou.

Thursday 12th May.

To-day we had a thrill and it actually made the majority of the ships company onboard rather apprehensive as to the outcome, "B" Guns crew went to drill, the first time that we had closed up a guns crew since we have been here, care was of course taken not to make the drill conspicuous to those onshore, but it did not evoke any excitement from the shore batteries.

1635 Aircraft overhead disappearing in the direction of Chin kiang.

Friday 13th May.

Lieut. Hett & But Sai Sin went ashore to interview Tai Ko Low. Interview was fruitless but Tai promised to telephone Nanking again. Suggested that Commanding Officer should send a letter to Nanking. Still no news of the wounded.

L st & S.B. No.	Name	Rating	Port Division and Official No.	Whence Entered	Date	Whither Discharged	Date

Friday 13ᵗʰ Cont.

Contractor again onboard and agreed to provide eggs at a reasonable price, but, stated that potatoes prohibitive owing to his inability to sell the sugar we exchanged for the last lot. It is of note that this is the first time that the side party sampan as been out to the ship since last Sunday forenoon.

Saturday 14ᵗʰ May.

There is noticeable increase in motor vessels moving up and down the river, they appeared to cause little excitment a the Control battery. Motor sampans first observed crossing the Yangtse ahead of the ship, a total of about twenty sun crossing to Grand Canal.

A Tug passing down river concealed its English name before passing Amethyst.

A fire was reported ahead of the ship at about 2230, it is possible that it is ammunition being burnt or could be fireworks. We had a visit from aircraft during the forenoon, but after passing overhead twice it carried on the way it was proceeding when first sighted.

Sunday 15ᵗʰ May.

Two sampans alongside with contractors from shore who brought us off some more potatoes.

Church service on the after mess deck, at which a prayer was said for our wounded ship mates, in fact this has been done every Sunday. May they have a speedy recovery.

Monday 16ᵗʰ May.

Weather very bad indeed today, blowing hard with occasional very heavy gusts, steam at immediate notice, we reverted to 2 hours at 1900 hours.

L st & S.B. No.	Name	Rating	Port Division and Official No.	Whence Entered	Date	Whither Discharged	Date

List & S.B. No.	Name	Rating	Port Division and Official No.	Whence Entered	Date	Whither Discharged	Date

Monday 16th Cont.

As both wind and sea (river) calmed down considerably. During the day the river was empty of traffic, later in the evening a few small tugs and junks were seen.

Tuesday 17th May.

Throughout the night convoys of lorries were observed passing along the road West-ward. Lt. Hett went ashore at 0900 to interview Tai Ko Liang, with a view to obtaining interview with the Area Commander at Chinkiang. The interview was satisfactory although T.K.L. would make no promises. Doctor treated the left eye of one of the sampan babies. 1700 T.K.L. came onboard to call on the Captain, this was done at the request of Lt Hett at the interview in the forenoon. He repeated that he could not get through by phone to the Area Commander as he was not "at home". He inferred that telephoning was very difficult and conversation had to be brief, this was offered as an excuse for failure to obtain information about the two wounded. This suggests that communication network is very much overworked and unreliable. He said that he would send a message with an "Aide Memoire" from Amethyst tonight and an interview might be possible in two to four days. Interview cordial.

Wednesday 18th May.

The C in C sent a signal hastening the safe conduct agreement.

Lt Hett went ashore to hasten interview with Col. Kang, the Area Commander at Chinkiang. Tai Ko Lou promised all cooperation and

L st & S.B. No.	Name	Rating	Port Division and Official No.	Whence Entered	Date	Whither Discharged	Date

18th May Cont.

would phone Chin Kiang P.M. if he did not receive a reply to request for interview at Chinkiang.

Later, T.K.L. and two political agents came onboard and delivered a reply to Amethyst's 3 Aide Memories. Interview lasted about 30 minutes and was cordial.

Weather deteriorated during the night.

Thursday 19th May.

Weather very bad this morning, blowing extra hard, ship came to immediate notice for steam, this lasted 5 hours from noon. No contact with shore today, owing to the weather. Battery off our Port bow apparently moved during the night, whilst it was dark.

Friday 20th May.

Battery off the Port Bow definately not visible this morning.

1700 Relief battery of horse or mule drawn Artillery, appear to have begun to dig themselves in, at the same emplacement on the Port bow, as the battery vacated last night, the guns appear to be about 12 pounders from here, but you can never tell. Certain amount of river traffic, but not much as the weather is still none to good.

Saturday 21st May.

Weather is much improved. Today we had the new battery squeesing the triggers of their guns both during the forenoon and evening, in fact I should say that they are that keen, they are actually trigger happy. Not much doing today.

L st & S.B. No.	Name	Rating	Port Division and Official No.	Whence Entered	Date	Whither Discharged	Date

List & S.B. No.	Name	Rating	Port Division and Official No.	Whence Entered	Date	Whither Discharged	Date

Sunday 22nd May.

Now, we are going to begin to feel the pinch, the fuel is getting low and we are having to shut down at night to try and be as economical as possible. We have emergency lighting run from our low power batteries, and it is suprising how the Electricians, have over come great difficulties to rig these emergency or secondary lighting arangements, we certainly owe them a vote of thanks.

0645 Power on the ship once more.

3 tugs came out of the Grand Canal at about 1400 towing about 40 craft between them, they appeared to be, motor sampans.

Shut down again for the night.

Monday 23rd May.

Further signal from the C in C for Col. Kang at Chiai Shan as been received. Lt Hett went ashore to bring off Tai Ko without effect. Later messenger from T.K.L. came onboard, to see if a message could be sent. Letter for the Col of the Battery, and area political agent was sent requesting that the C in C's note be personally delivered to the General.

Three heavy guns which were mounted on barges, were towed down the Grand Canal at about 1130 this forenoon.

Same routine as for steam.

Tuesday 24th May.

During the forenoon 3 timber rafts were towed down river, and this is certainly a work of art, in this river.

The sampan went inshore and brought a letter back to the ship, which, stated that an

L st & S.B. No.	Name	Rating	Port Division and Official No.	Whence Entered	Date	Whither Discharged	Date

List & S.B. No.	Name	Rating	Port Division and Official No.	Whence Entered	Date	Whither Discharged	Date

Tuesday 24th Cont

interview had been arranged between Col. Kang
and the Captain. Captain then went ashore
to deliver to Col. Kang the C. in C's note.
and returned at about 1830. routine for steam.

Wednesday 25th May.

Lt Hett went ashore during the forenoon
to deliver formal request for the return
of the two wounded ratings. They had
promised at the meeting the day before to
return them on receiving a formal request
in writing.

Contractor came onboard to barter food.
arrangements were made for him to supply
us with eggs and potatoes.

Electrician Blomley went ashore to deliver
to T.K.L. a letter for the Col. giving the
C in C's request that Amethyst be supplied
with provisions & fuel.

At about 1715 sampan brought a note
from T.K.L. saying that the two wounded
are onshore. Lt Hett went ashore to
collect & bring them off to the ship.
1815 Sampan returned, S.M. Bannister &
Boy Martin returned to the ship. Stated
that they had been well treated with
plenty of food, if not always as they
would have liked it.

Thursday 26th May.

No communication with the shore, although
the sampan was alongside. Sampan hailed
from shore, went, but did not return to
the ship, called in by the contractor.
Weather very bad again.

Mr Leo interpretor to Naval Attachee Nanking, arrived
in the village and remained with Tai Kou Wang.

L st & S.B. No.	Name	Rating	Port Division and Official No.	Whence Entered	Date	Whither Discharged	Date

List & S.B. No.	Name	Rating	Port Division and Official No.	Whence Entered	Date	Whither Discharged	Date

Friday 27th May.

Sampan came out to the ship bringing fresh vegetables & eggs. Weather still bad, consequently we have not seen much river traffic.

Saturday 28th May.

Today the weather is too bad, we definately cannot establish communication with shore, in fact there have only been 3 or 4 fishing junks out all day, and it is bad when they stop.

Sunday 29th May.

Well if I remember rightly at home, this is Royal Oak Day, gee I wish that I was back in that old English village where I was born, but one never knows, one of these days perhaps we shall be moving off down river. The weather has improved a lot. Electrician Blomley went ashore with the C in C's despatch. Returned onboard and brought some mail from Nanking.

Mr Leo the interpretor joined the ship today.

Monday 30th May.

Today as been uneventful. The weather is very poor. Large floating timber raft, proceeding down river, secured to the Port bank off our Port bow for the night. I am afraid that the out look is beginning to get grim.

Tuesday 31st May.

Another uneventful night and forenoon. After lunch a ferry brought Col. Kang and his wingers down river and landed them ashore on our Port beam, about half an hour later it came out to the ship to take the Captain to

L st & S.B. No.	Name	Rating	Port Division and Official No.	Whence Entered	Date	Whither Discharged	Date

31st May Cont.

a meeting with Kang. Captain returned onboard, shut down steam after signal had been passed to C in C. detailing the result of the meeting.

Wednesday 1st June.

The raft which had been moored to the bank off our Port bow, sailed with one tug down river at 0915. The remainder of the day was uneventful.

Thursday 2nd June.

In the early morning two large lighters went down river being towed by a medium sized tug named "Pei-Kiang" of Shanghai. Later in the forenoon two lighters with Reg No. 331 & 332 towed by tug named "Cheng Sang" went down river. Mr Leo our interpretor went ashore to talk with Tai Kou Wang, he also spoke to Col. Kang by telephone. During the afternoon 11 M.L's. & 5 L.C.M's. passed the ship going down river and entered the canal at Chen Po Chien Kow, Chinese Naval (Nationalist) Officers and ratings were seen in most of the vessels.

During the evening the battery fired one round a a tug ferry coming up the river without flying the proper flag, but this was very soon hoisted and carried on her journey unharmed. It appears that the code flags for ship moving in the river is a red & green flag. Ships proceeding up river have the red flag hoisted superior to the green & coming down river the position is reversed.

Friday 3rd June.

At about 1030 a launch called at the South Bank and collected Tai Kou Lou and then came out to the ship to ask the Captain to

L st & S.B. No.	Name	Rating	Port Division and Official No.	Whence Entered	Date	Whither Discharged	Date

List & S.B. No.	Name	Rating	Port Division and Official No.	Whence Entered	Date	Whither Discharged	Date

Friday 3rd Cont.

attend an interview with Col. Kang at Chias Shan, the Captain agreed and went ashore in the launch, returning at about 1830, and not looking to happy about things, and we found out later that he was not.

Saturday 4th June.

Early morning two motor lighters Chi-kin & Chin Chen passed down river. About an hour later a large tug named the "Ming" & numbered 306 with large lighter secured alongside proceeded down river.

Contractor came onboard during the forenoon to arrange supply of potatoes & eggs.

Mr Leo left the ship on his way to Nanking to collect 200,000 Chen Ming (P.L.A. money) from the Naval Attachée there.

Sunday 5th June

Both the weather & visibility deteriorated during the afternoon, and it was not to pleasant doing a watch on the bridge.

A Gunboat passed the ship going up river mounting a small calibre (·303 or 300) in an Orlikon mounting, gun was pointed at the ship but unmanned as craft passed Amethyst.

Monday 6th June.

Traffic now back to normal on river, we had one large passenger steamer pass us going up river, the MING CHUAN registered at Shanghai.

Weather very bad and getting worse. Shut down at 2030 but at 2230 we had to flash up again and go to immediate notice, owing to the weather.

Tuesday 7th June.

Rough night, blowing hard and raining.

L st & S.B. No.	Name	Rating	Port Division and Official No.	Whence Entered	Date	Whither Discharged	Date

Tuesday 7th Cont.

Later, reverted to 4 hours notice for steam.
Tug TR CHUAN towing a large covered in barge
full of civilians passed the ship proceeding
down river. During the afternoon the contractors
came onboard with eggs. Uneventful day.

Wednesday 8th June.

Nothing happened during the night. At 0800
approx. 100 soldiers were observed marching
along the main road on the South Bank.
Gunboat with 20 soldiers onboard passed the
ship (and slowed down whilst passing) going up
river, they definately appeared to be on a
sight seeing trip. This gunboat returned
at about 1230 doing the same thing but on
the opposite side of the ship.
A gale blew up at 1730 which was most
unexpected as there was not a cloud in the
sky one minute and then it was blowing
and raining like hell, and it subsided
just as quickly in about 3/4's of an hour.
Shut down at 1910. We are even getting used
to this now.

Thursday 9th June.

Kings birthday, but not for Amethyst, no flags,
no holiday, no salute in fact no nothings.
It looks like being a nice day but after 8 weeks
in the Yangtse, we have learnt to our cost,
that it can be very deceptive. We learnt by
signal today that our mail has reached
Shanghai, and that the Air Attaché Howard Williams
is going to try and bring it up for us by jeep.
Good Luck, to the air force, we already have one
of there doctors staying with us, and how thankful
we are that he is here. A tug towing two barges
both with there reg. nos in English 303 & 304 passed
us going down river.

L st & S.B. No.	Name	Rating	Port Division and Official No.	Whence Entered	Date	Whither Discharged	Date

List & S.B. No.	Name	Rating	Port Division and Official No.	Whence Entered	Date	Whither Discharged	Date

Friday 10th June.

Another uneventful night, the frogs are croaking all night long, on the beaches each side of the river and we hear the cuckoo at all hours of the night, in fact, it makes you think that you are home again on a fine spring morning, until, you take a look around and see all the sampans out fishing, and believe me this is hard work on this river. The contractor came onboard this morning with potatoes & cabbage, but it is not a bit like we get in U.K. Still we have to be thankful for what we can get, because, without them we should be in a very bad way. Over the radio we hear that the communist Mayor of Shanghai is appealing for trade. It is a glorious day, slight breeze blowing and plenty of sun. The control battery on our Port bow fired small arms at an ex-L.C.1 towing a barge & going up river, and made her go over from the north to the south bank for inspection, the L.C.1 was flying the flags of the international code and after about a half hour delay, she was allowed to proceed up river. Mr Leo returned from Nanking and brought a parcel of books and a private letter for me from my very good friends Flt Sgt & Mrs Jack Scarbough. Some day I may be able to thank them for their kindness & let them know just how the letter, and books were appreciated both by myself and the rest of the boys. Mr Leo was held ashore at C.P.L.B. H.Q's because his pass was for four days and he had taken five, as he had to wait for our money, 200,000 CHEN MIN. (Communist currency) which when he got it was quoted at 580 to the £, but the next day it was 2,800 and therefore as all Chinese currency useless. They soon let him return onboard.

L st & S.B. No.	Name	Rating	Port Division and Official No.	Whence Entered	Date	Whither Discharged	Date

List & S.B. No.	Name	Rating	Port Division and Official No.	Whence Entered	Date	Whither Discharged	Date

Saturday 11th June.

Another lovely day. The usual amount of traffic on the river. During the afternoon one L.S.T. passed down river with some soldiers of the C.P.L.A. and women onboard who had the audacity to wave to us onboard Amethyst as they passed by. Our side party sampan went ashore and brought two soldiers out, who took photographs off the ship.

Sunday 12th June.

Quiet and uneventful night. Launch came to the ship from shore containing soldiers, one of whom had a letter from Col. Kang.

At 1045 the Captain, Store P.O. McCarthy & Mr Leo, went ashore for interview.

The Captain informed Col Kang that the question of safe conduct was being dealt with by higher level authorities in Peiping and Nanking. Col stated that he knew nothing about that, but by the end of the interview had promised to to telephone both Peiping and Nanking for information. Also stated that the General would be only too pleased to give a pass for the mail to be brought through from Shanghai, but must arrange it with other authorities first. Repeated his statement of previous interview that he would give every assistance in Amethyst obtaining fresh provisions.

He told the Captain that he had no objection to Amethyst proceeding down river, providing that Peiping & Nanking gave him the orders. This would of course save his face and put him 'right in the clear. He did not say that, it is only my own thoughts.

Monday 13th June.

Uneventful but very unpleasant night, blowing hard and raining until about 0400, then it

L st & S.B. No.	Name	Rating	Port Division and Official No.	Whence Entered	Date	Whither Discharged	Date

13ᵗʰ CONT

cleared up. Later still blowing but the sun is now shining. At 1445 the KIANG HSIN proceeding ~~down river~~ up river with passengers. This was the first ship, since we have been anchored here to give the Maritime Courtesy of the sea. (That is the dipping of the ensigns).

Still we get the surprises only half an hour later, a ship proceeding down river the KIANG-AN passed the Courtesy of the sea. She was also wearing two very large photographs ~~with~~ which took the whole of the front of the bridge of the Chairman of the C.P.L.A. MAO TSE TONG and she also dressed ship from bow to the top of her foremast, with two strings of red flags, which were lowered just as she had passed us. About 300 soldiers observed to be carrying out exercises on the hills opposite the ship during the evening. We are now beginning to look with anxious eyes to the oil readings every morning as it is beginning to get very low.

Tuesday. 14ᵗʰ June.

The night as been uneventful. Dawn broke with the Cookoo in full song, the sun shining, but the wind still very strong. This evening a large converted T.L.C. passed and the Maritime courtesy of the sea was exchanged between the two ships. Shut down engine & boiler rooms for 24 hours. Flash up again at 0730 on Thursday morning.

Wednesday 15ᵗʰ June

Very bad night; pouring with rain throughout. Today we are starting our real test of of economy, there will be no power on the ship at all until tomorrow, all water for drinking and washing will be pumped by hand and to

L st & S.B. No.	Name	Rating	Port Division and Official No.	Whence Entered	Date	Whither Discharged	Date

15th cont.

flush the lavatory's water will be pumped by hand from the Yangtze. The Captain went ashore this morning and he has now returned onboard but what the outcome of this will be it is impossible to tell yet. Everyone seems to be taking this grim situation in their stride and showing all the usual attitudes of indifference, which in fact is the attitude of the British sailor everywhere. He swears and raves and lets himself go and forgets for a while at least everything that is going on. It is now 57 days since we first found ourselves in this unhappy situation, and it certainly does not seem as if we are any nearer to getting down the Yangtze and away from here than we were 50 days ago.

Thursday 16th June '49.

To night as been the exact opposite to last night. The Captain cleared lower deck and gave us the outline of yesterdays meeting. And taking all points it seems to have got just about as far as any of the previous ones. Col. KANG will not go to Nanking or Shanghai for any meetings, they must be held here. The Captain drove home to Col Kang at last, that a person with the rank of an Admiral in the Royal Navy, who is also the Commander-in-Chief of the Far Eastern Station is not in the habit of falsifying statements, and that if Col Kang was not prepared to apologise to the Admiral or come to some other arrangements, he, the Admiral would have nothing more to do with Col Kang through these channels. Actually in so many words it meant a win for us in this

L st & S.B. No.	Name	Rating	Port Division and Official No.	Whence Entered	Date	Whither Discharged	Date

16<u>th</u> Cont.

round, because he is allowing Captain Donaldson the Naval Attaché at Nanking to represent the British Navy in these talks now, with of course the Admirals permission. It seems that Kang definately does not want to go to a higher level, for the very simple reason that if he cannot deal with it himself here and come to some agreement soon, he might possibly have to go. When told about the hardship & discomfort he is causing to the Ship company of H.M.S. Amethyst, he said " that he had at various times offered to help the ship in various ways." He has granted the Boy with the suspected broken arm a safe passage with the doctor to Chinkiang for an X ray. As for our mail which is waiting for us in Shanghai, he is getting in touch with the Foreign Bureau to see what they are doing about it. The interview was rather stormy. After it was over and they brought the Captain & Interpreter back to the ship, they took a trip round the ship having a look at the damage they had done. This is the first time that Col Kang has been anywhere near the ship.

Friday 17<u>th</u> June

Captain today sent a letter to Col Kang asking when it would be convenient for the Boy with the broken arm to go for his X ray, as the Doctor thinks this should be done now. Well this evening we had a real bit of excitment our first for days, a large passenger steamer came down river, passed by us and then turned and proceeded back up river until it got abreast of Amethyst,

L st & S.B. No.	Name	Rating	Port Division and Official No.	Whence Entered	Date	Whither Discharged	Date

List & S.B. No.	Name	Rating	Port Division and Official No.	Whence Entered	Date	Whither Discharged	Date

17th CONT.

and then dropped anchor, this being the first
vessel to anchor anywhere near here, since we
arrived. One other item, the battery off our
port bow seem to have evacuated, as when this
ship anchored, there was not a soldier in sight
on the cliff and usually when any ship goes
up or down river there is about 50 of them
and the guns are manned. That is all for
today but will ascertain the name of the
ship at day-light tomorrow.

Saturday 18th June.
The China Steam Navigation Co's passenger ship
"Ming Ling" left at day break and proceeded
up river. This is now our 60 day here,
how many more we are likely to stay - God
alone knows. This evening we saw the largest
cargo vessel yet to proceed either up or down
river, a vessel of about four thousand tons,
and loaded right down to her plimsol mark,
she was drawing 27 ft of water. Also she
appeared to be taking no chances whatever with
the communist batterys or the national air force,
as she was heavily protected with sand bags
around the bridge & had small trees at the
mast-head & yard-arms, top of the bridge - funnel
& what is thought on ship to be the most
vulnerable points open to air-craft. Shortly after
this a fully laden oil tanker passed by, how we
wished that she would come alongside, as things
are now beginning to get very uncomfortable, with
no lights or anything for 24 hours about & it is
going to be much worse before long. The Captain
went ashore for an interview, Col Kang wanted to know
if the C. in C. had appointed a deputy yet? but the
Captain with true diplomatic forethought answered, "it

L st & S.B. No.	Name	Rating	Port Division and Official No.	Whence Entered	Date	Whither Discharged	Date

List & S.B. No.	Name	Rating	Port Division and Official No.	Whence Entered	Date	Whither Discharged	Date

18th Cont.

is being considered," although we knew even then, that Capt. Donaldson had already been appointed, if he was required. Boy Horton can have an X ray on Monday.

Sunday 19th June.

Uneventful and quiet night. This looks as if it may develope into the hottest day we have had so far, as it is really hot now at 1000 hours. Owing to there being no lights or fans on the mess deck, Church was held at 1100 hours on the Quarter-deck at which Lt. K.S. Hett read the lesson. It did turn out to be our hottest day & we knew it alright.

Monday 20th June.

We had a new thing happened to us today, well it is new so far as we are concerned, the ships company aired their bedding, as it was a lovely day, and of course depending on what bedding they have? Then we had a medical inspection by our R.A.F. doctor, thank heavens that he got onboard here, but what a time to spend here with us, still we are all most grateful to him (Flt Lieut. Yearnley, R.A.F) for everything he has done to keep us all in good health. We are having a damage control course for the boys and this morning the Captain gave the introduction speech to commence the course. It is now two months since we ran into this trouble of ours and up to now we look like remaining another two?

The Captain went ashore at the request of the Gen. General Yuan Chung-Hsien for a meeting at C.P.L.A. H.Q's. at Chin-Kiang, apparently the meeting although on cordial terms, was not entirely satisfactory, although for about the first time there is a ray (small) of hope beginning to gleam from

L st & S.B. No.	Name	Rating	Port Division and Official No.	Whence Entered	Date	Whither Discharged	Date

List & S.B. No.	Name	Rating	Port Division and Official No.	Whence Entered	Date	Whither Discharged	Date

behind that dark "iron curtain". The Gen. will allow our mail to come through, but how it comes is up to Shanghai entirely, that is a true picture of this C.P.L.A. no one wants the responsibility of making a decision on their own.

Boy 1st Class S. Horton went ashore for an X ray this evening and returned by boat from ChinKiang later this evening.

Tuesday 21st June.

Weather very hot indeed, certainly later it proved to be the hottest day so far. Two ratings today caught the sun & for their trouble got a slight attack of diarrhea and a very high temperature.

Wednesday 22nd June.

Dawn broke nice this morning, after a quiet night, cookoo still singing and a nice steady breeze, but what it will develope into, is hard to tell up the Yangtse. The Interpretor is going ashore, but as yet the Captain as not said what for. Later P.M., the Captain went ashore for a meeting, which by all accounts was a huge success, in fact it was the first meeting at which the talk had been really straight throughout. The General agreed to our mail being sent from Shanghai, addressed to him at his H.Q's in ChinKiang, and he would have it collected and sent to the ship by boat.

Thursday 23rd June.

Captain cleared lower deck for a talk on the outcome of yesterdays meeting. The Gen. very pointedly said that he could not even think of a merchant ship coming from Hong Kong to replenish us with fuel & stores. But if the C in C would send to him (the Gen) a letter or signal

L st & S.B. No.	Name	Rating	Port Division and Official No.	Whence Entered	Date	Whither Discharged	Date

List & S.B. No.	Name	Rating	Port Division and Official No.	Whence Entered	Date	Whither Discharged	Date

23ʳᵈ Cont

stating that the British warship (singular) had entered
the C.P.L.A. battlefront indiscriminately we could
proceed down river or at least he would consider
it. The Captain finished his talk by saying that
I, the coxswain would accompany him to the
next meeting.

Friday 24th June.
A lot cooler today, Mr Leo with one unofficial
chinese laundry boy as gone ashore with the
intention if possible of collecting our mail,
which as been despatched through the Shanghai
Postal Services, he will stay ashore until
it does arrive at Ching Kiang. The usual
amount of river traffic operating, inspite of
the Nationalist bombing outrage and statement
that they are blockading all communist held
ports from now on. The first ship we have
seen during the night passed by at 0245 this
morning. The mail did arrive at midnight.
I got a rude awakening to sort it out.

Saturday 25th June
Great rejoicing today, everyone talking about the
different accounts of our encounter with the
communist battery, and re-reading of mail.
Mr Leo went ashore with a letter from Captain
to Col Kang and he had to stay ashore
all night owing to the weather.
The mail which we received last night was the
first (1) for 70 days

Sunday 26th June.
What a night, after shutting down, we had to
flash up again at 0100 as the weather got so
bad. We received the C in C's signal last night
in reply to the General, and we are all now
in high hopes that Amethyst will soon be allowed

L st & S.B. No.	Name	Rating	Port Division and Official No.	Whence Entered	Date	Whither Discharged	Date

List & S.B. No.	Name	Rating	Port Division and Official No.	Whence Entered	Date	Whither Discharged	Date

26ᵗʰ CONT.

to depart. There have been a lot of false stories in the national papers regarding the ship. I am afraid that quite a lot of the facts are far from true. Of course we realize that the people that gave them could not have the facts really clear as they themselves had been through that hell and then gone ashore. We can only hope that the Admiralty informed our next of kin ~~were informed~~ before these stories appeared in the national papers? Still very rough, no contact with shore.

Monday 27ᵗʰ June.

Still very rough, but the weather is ~~still~~ easing down now. There is still no contact with shore. Mᵗ Leo has been ashore since saturday. We are now without power until 0500 on Wednesday morning, as we have to cut our fuel consumption drastically now to make it go as far as possible. Our sampan came down river on the south bank and a soldier got onboard at the usual landing place, they got half way across and then had to turn back as it was too rough, with the wind and tide against one another.

Tuesday 28ᵗʰ June.

Another rough night, but at last the wind is now dying down. Mᵗ Leo and one C.P.L.A soldier came onboard in a fishing junk. Mᵗ Leo went ashore again with a letter from the Captain. A very sad blow today, the Captain is ~~too~~ ill and is spending the day in bed, his illness is due to this very inclement weather, and dampness of the ship owing to having no power for these 48 hour periods. We trust that he will soon be about again as

L st & S.B. No.	Name	Rating	Port Division and Official No.	Whence Entered	Date	Whither Discharged	Date
L st & S.B. No.	Name	Rating	Port Division and Official No.	Whence Entered	Date	Whither Discharged	Date

28<u>th</u> CONT

without him we are lost.

Wednesday 29<u>th</u> June.

I am very pleased to be able say that the Captain, is a little better today and he does expect to be able to go ashore if there is a meeting. We have flashed up today, until ten o'clock this evening. Time certainly marches on, it is now 71 days since we left Shanghai. Perhaps I shall be able to report more movement after I have been ashore with the Captain. — More disappointment, there will be no meeting today.

Thursday 30<u>th</u> June.

Weather is still bad, and so is the Captain. Later no meeting again today, owing to the General being away from Ching Kiang, no one seems to know where he is gone. Still raining like hell but it looks like clearing. — This is the last day of the first half of the year and our 72 day here, I wonder how many more we are going to have? Captain Tye, political adviser to the local Commander came onboard to see the Captain, this morning. After he had gone the Captain cleared lower deck. The news he gave us was of the worst, the General will allow us to have the oil down from Nanking and that is all. There can be no meeting for (7) seven days owing to the fact that the C.P.L.A. are very busy arranging for 7 days of victory parades, which commence tomorrow the 1<u>st</u> July. So we have just got to sit here and wait. My own firm believe is that they are holding us here now so that they can use us as propaganda during this forth coming C.P.L.A. week, and that

L st & S.B. No.	Name	Rating	Port Division and Official No.	Whence Entered	Date	Whither Discharged	Date
L st & S.B. No.			Port Division and Official No.	Whence Entered		Whither Discharged	Date

List & S.B. No.	Name	Rating	Port Division and Official No.	Whence Entered	Date	Whither Discharged	Date

30<u>TH</u> CONT.

in fact the General is holding the answer to the Admirals letter, till this is all over? There is just one thing now that is quite certain and is the fact that they cannot now accuse either our Captain or the C in C of trying to frustrate there efforts to arrange things for us.

Mr Leo & the Leading Cook (Chinese) have gone ashore to meet Mr Khoong of the A.N.A^c staff Shanghai, who is bringing a parcel of stores for us, including charts & money. Midnight they have still not returned, although he was supposed to arrive at 1400 hours this afternoon.

Friday 1<u>st</u> July.

A large ex-T.L.C went up river during the night, so it looks as if they are now allowing night traffic on the river. Very quiet day. Mr Leo returned with the stores from Shanghai, but the C.P.L.A. H.Q's. would not allow the charts of the Yangtse river to come onboard, obviously they don't trust us? little do they know that we can go down without them. I received a personal letter from C.P.O. Cunningham (A.N.A's Staff Shanghai) in which he said they had a real hard time getting our mail through, and if it was not for spoiling any chance we might have of getting away from here shortly, he would come up as a chinese, in the ordinary way. I fully believe that he could and would, as he can speak Chinese like a native and better than some.

Saturday 2<u>nd</u> July.

A little excitement during the night when a ship coming up river came that close everyone awake thought that she was going to ram us, but at the last moment she put her

L st & S.B. No.	Name	Rating	Port Division and Official No.	Whence Entered	Date	Whither Discharged	Date

2ᴺᴰ CONT.

helm over and just missed us. We are not allowed to stow any lights during the dark hours in case the Nationalists decide to send there air force on a bombing raid up this way. It does not appear as though the Captain will get another meeting before the 8ᵗʰ July, that is putting it at the very earliest. Then it may be a fortnight before we can proceed down river. Still my guess is the 18ᵗʰ July, that date incidently will be exactly 3 months, so heres hoping.

Sunday 3ʳᵈ June.

Still another ship nearly rammed us again during the night, this is getting rather to much, our nerves are not in a condition to stand many shocks like that these days. But now the Captain as ordered anchor light forward and stern light aft to be stown during the dark hours. Today we heard a programme of records played for us by the B.B.C. in listeners choice, request programme. Conditions were excellent and we heard it loud & clear, we all really enjoyed it, but I think the first one was the masterpiece, "A life on the ocean wave," played for Flt. Lt. Yearnley our R.A.F doctor.

Monday 4ᵗʰ July.

All was quiet in our area of the Yangtse during the night, and except for the usual river traffic it has been uneventful today. The ships company are still in good spirits, inspite of everything.

Tuesday 5ᵗʰ July.

The Captain was called ashore for a meeting with Col. Kang, which I am very pleased to be able to say that I attended, not only

L st & S.B. No.	Name	Rating	Port Division and Official No.	Whence Entered	Date	Whither Discharged	Date
	Please Note. Petty Officer Frank's Notes and full report are at the back of this Diary.					⟶	

List & S.B. No.	Name	Rating	Port Division and Official No.	Whence Entered	Date	Whither Discharged	Date

5th CONT.

just to have been at one of these meetings, but because it gave me an insight of how the diplomatic service really works, and our Captain, Lt. Com. Kerans, is truely one of the best. I might say again, that whatever is the outcome of this meeting, and it might mean our early release! we could not have done without him, in fact I might had, without fear of contradiction, that if it had not been for him & Lieut (L) Strain, the remaining crew of the "Amethyst" would have been down hearted after the first couple of weeks, but between them they have kept the moral really high, with their cheerfulness & spirit and most of all tact, at times when things have not been going too well.

We went astore to this meeting in a real down four of rain, but that did not damp our spirit because we went astore full of hope that the end was insight. When we returned we had a feeling that the next meeting would be the final one, and that soon after that we shall be able to sail. But more about the meeting and a fuller report with the notes which I took are on separate sheets attached to this.

6th - 7th & 8th July.

Very bad weather as prevailed for the last three days and it is rather depressing as our fuel is now getting to the point where we might have to shut down altogether, inspite of the fact that Col Kang is telephoning to Nanking to tell them to hurry with the arrangements for our oil. In fact we have had a signal

L.st & S.B. No.	Name	Rating	Port Division and Official No.	Whence Entered	Date	Whither Discharged	Date

List & S.B. No.	Name	Rating	Port Division and Official No.	Whence Entered	Date	Whither Discharged	Date

6ᵗʰ 7ᵗʰ 8ᵗʰ Cont.

to say that it as been sent, so we can only presume that it is held up by the weather?

Saturday 9ᵗʰ July.

Today everyone is keeping a good lookout up river, watching for a tug towing a lighter with oil drums onboard as the weather is much improved. At last the tug has been sighted and it is now trying to get alongside our Starboard side, but it is fighting a losing battle as the tide is to strong and inspite of all its valiant efforts it is slowly but surely drifting away down stream.

The tug and junk are now alongside, 296 drums of oil about 60 tons, what a God send, the sight of it there is a very great stimulant to all on board, although they know that it means 24 tons damned hard work getting it inboard. We cannot start oiling until tomorrow as it is to dangerous to start in the dark.

We have had a set back now which makes a hell of a difference to our stay here, our emergency Wireless set, which works from the battery and which we have been using when we shut down as at last broke down, the last and only valve we had for it as given out, which means that we can now only transmit when we are flashed up. So that is another reason that we are more cheerful that the oil as arrived.

Sunday 10ᵗʰ July.

0500, The hands have commenced "Operation Oil", 296 drums of it, all to be hoisted inboard and drained into the oil fuel tank by hand.

L st & S.B. No.	Name	Rating	Port Division and Official No.	Whence Entered	Date	Whither Discharged	Date

List & S.B. No.	Name	Rating	Port Division and Official No.	Whence Entered	Date	Whither Discharged	Date

10th CONT.

Later everything is working smoothly and very satisfactory. Noon if we can carry on at the same speed we shall be finished by about 1800 hours, all are doing a great job. Everyone now working like hell to get finished as soon as possible, oil all over the place, everyone covered in the stuff, but no one cares "Operation Oil" is now finished, at 1600 hours all inboard and in the tanks. The impossible as been done, what an achievement, a feat that I should think is without parallel in the history of our ~~glorious~~ glorious Navy.

The Captain sent the following to C in C.

"Fuel now onboard 54 tons, operation commenced 0500, finished at 1600 hours, working nonstop throughout, 11 hours. They worked like TROJANS."

What makes this all the more praise worthy, is the fact that not only have the ship company had no exercise for 82 days but everything used in this operation had to be improvised. Then to make everyone just a little bit happier the Captain got a letter asking him to attend a meeting tomorrow the 11th at C.P.L.A. H.Q's. Chingkiang, which generally means that the General will be there.

We are hoping and I might say quietly confident that this will be the last?

Monday 11th July.

We all had a lay in this morning after the great effort of yesterday, I might had that no one needed much rocking to sleep last night, in fact the whole ship was very very quiet at about 9-30.

Now everyone is wondering what is going to happen today at the meeting?

L st & S.B. No.	Name	Rating	Port Division and Official No.	Whence Entered	Date	Whither Discharged	Date

11th Cont.

The Captain & Lt(L) Strain have just returned onboard and I regret to say that things are not to good in fact, I should go so far as to say they are grim.

We have been informed that we go on half rations from tomorrow 12th, so it looks as if the Captain thinks that they are going to try to starve us in to giving in and using the wording they want us to? But then again Kang does not know the British sailor, and whatever the Captain decides he can rest assured that we are all with him, and we shall not let him down.

Tuesday 12th July.

Today we are not quite so joyful or should I say cheerful? but that is bound to be the feeling for a day, you see every one was so keyed up that the result of yesterdays meeting is a sort of anti-climax to every-thing. We are now on Half Rations. The Captain has just had a talk with the ships company and explained to us what happened at yesterdays meeting. Apparently although he asked Col Kang he could not get a meeting with the General, in fact this was absolutely impossible? only because Kang did not want him to see him, this of course is only my own opinion. When asked about replenishments by ship, Kang stated that no foreign merchant ships were allowed up the Yangtse, and if, any ship or plane attempted to go near "Amethyst" it would be destroyed. And again the Captain was threatened with destruction if he attempted to move the ship. I think Kang must think the Captain

L st & S.B. No.	Name	Rating	Port Division and Official No.	Whence Entered	Date	Whither Discharged	Date

List & S.B. No.	Name	Rating	Port Division and Official No.	Whence Entered	Date	Whither Discharged	Date

12TH CONT.

Officers and ships company remaining onboard "Amethyst" are mad. The whole deadlock of the meeting, is when boiled down, that Kang will not accept a signal from the C in C with our Captains counter signature as he says that it is not legal. And he wants a letter from the C in C. in his own hand writing, which is all rubbish, with the C in C in Japan.

My own opinion of this, is that during the seven days celebrations he as been in contact with a few extremists and this as gone to his head, as he told our Captain that 450,000,000 Chinese were looking to him Kang to clear the situation, which is of course utter rubbish, and the Captain proved that he is a real diplomat by not replying to that. They are also blaming him for the entry of Lieut. G.L. Weston into Ching Kiang whilst trying to return to the ship from Shanghai.

In vain the Captain tried to point out that Weston was under the orders of the Shanghai police and that he the Captain had sent a letter to Kang as soon as he heard that he was coming. Then Kang came back with, what right had British Military personnel to be travelling on Chinese soil? The Captain again refrained from answering. Kang seems to think that we do intend to try and move, as his interpretor told Mr Leo to leave the ship before it did move, as it would certainly be destroyed.

Wednesday 13th July.

We are all settling down now to the thought of half rations, in fact after the first 24 hours we dont seem to be doing to bad, still it is much better

L st & S.B. No.	Name	Rating	Port Division and Official No.	Whence Entered	Date	Whither Discharged	Date

List & S.B. No.	Name	Rating	Port Division and Official No.	Whence Entered	Date	Whither Discharged	Date

13ᵗʰ Cont.

to commence now than wait and find ourselves with
hardly anything left at all; there is one definate
thing and that is we shall not starve. This as
been another dull & dreary day.

At about 1940 the soldiers ashore stopped a sampan
and made it go into the shore, they held it
there until after nine o'clock and at about
9-20 we saw it coming across to the ship, when
it arrived alongside, Capt Tai Ko Low ——— the
Political Adviser to the Garrison Commander locally
came onboard and told Mr Leo he had
letters for the Captain. I don't know but I
should think it was rather important? otherwise
I think they would have waited until the
morning? At 9-25 the Captain ordered the
engine room to flash up again in order to
send a signal to the C in C.

       Thursday 14ᵗʰ July.

The Captain is clearing lower deck at 1035,
presumably to squash the rumours that are going
round the ship, which of course are inevitable
whenever a letter or soldier comes onboard.
And we hope, that he will have some news
for us? Well the Captain spoke to us for
about 15 minutes and mostly about security, which
is quiet right, the whole thing boils down to
the fact that people talk onboard and although
we cannot go ashore, we have Chinese onboard
and they hear things and pass them on to
the girls in the sampan and they in turn
talk to the people when they get ashore.
The brightest thing is that eventually the letters
which the Captain left ashore have got through
to the General. And now he is accusing the
Captain or the British side of using delaying

NOTICE BOARD ISSUE.
****

Following message has just been received :-

Addressed to "Amethyst"   repeated   All Authorities Ashore and Afloat on
                                        The Far East Station.

                                            from CinCFES(Afloat).

                        Following is a message for all in "Amethyst".

2. For many reason your situation is NOT recieving publicity at the moment,
but I can assure you that you are very much in the mind of the Government and
people at Home. In fact the eyes of the World are upon you. All your Fleet
mates are particularily concerned with your future and no effort is being
spared to help you in any way that appears possible .

3. It is clear that the Communists have been holding you hostage to bring
admissions from the British Government which would not only be untrue and
dishonourable but would harm the cause of free Nations in the future.

4. For the present therefore you are in the forefront of what is called the
"cold war" in which the cause of freedom is being attacked. I know it is a
pretty hot war so far as you are concerned and your stand is widely recognised
and greatly admired.

5. No one can yet say how this will all end, but of one thing I am quite sure,
neither The British Government, The Amethyst's Ship's Company nor myself
will ever submit to threats, insults or perversions of the truth ; nor shall we
do anything to harm our country's honour .

6. You are always in our thoughts and I hope the accumulated good wishes of so
many of us will cheer you up and give you confidence.

                            DTG 140825 Z July,1949.

I have also just had the following message from the Commander-in-Chief in the
text of another message.
            " I hear the Admiralty are sending regular letters to
next-of-kin of all onboard to keep them informed so far as possible of your
situation".

            KEEP THIS NOTICE CLEAN SO ALL CAN READ.
            ****

    Distribution:- Main Notice Boards.
                    Stokers Messes.
                    Petty Officers Messes.
                    File.

14th July,1949.

14th Cont

tactics, but this of course is a series of lies, by which they hope to stampede our Captain into a false move, but I am afraid that they will not do that. Now we are awaiting the C in C's next move. Kang is allowing our stores to come through and is giving every assistance in getting them to the ship. "So he says". Just like the mail which was well searched, before it eventually reached the ship. The C in C has addressed a letter to all onboard the "Amethyst" and every one in the Far Eastern Station and the Captain as just had it put on the notice boards for our perusal, a copy is attached to this page.

Friday 15th July.

I forgot to put in yesterdays piece that the contractors had brought some potatoes, cabbage, eggs and even peaches, and a thing that none of us expected as Kang had stopped them coming onboard once was matches.

Well I have been working since 0225, I had a rather rude awakening just before then when one of the boys came in from the bridge with a chit from the Captain, and as I had to go on watch at 0500 I thought I had better get it finished as I have to see the Captain at 0700. The job I had to do was all wrong, so I had to do it the right way, still it is finished now.

Mr Leo went ashore this afternoon to collect stores from Shanghai.

Saturday 16th July.

Rather quiet today, usual saturday routine, Captains rounds of the messdecks, which I am pleased to say are being kept in a

NAVAL MESSAGE.

Unclassified.
****

To: From:

CinCFES(Afloat) repeated F3,FO2i/cFES(Afloat)   AMETHYST.

(The following signal is in reply to CinC's message which was on the notice
boards yesterday)

Thank you indeed for your 140825.

2). I quote from my S.181 (which is the Quarterly Punishment Return)
on the 30th June and is as true as ever.

3). Quote ..I cannot speak too highly of the conduct,bearing and fortitude
of my remaining Ship's Company. They have endured a long period of
hardships under almost intolerable conditions , with cheerfulness and
courage, which can have few equals in time of peace. Many of them are
now arrivals on the Station and nearly all extremely young.
British spirit in adversity has once again shown itself to be unassailable.

4). This return has been Blank since the incident.

5). Please tell the Fleet we shall keep the old flag flying, riddled though
it may be by gunfire, and come what may.
Good luck to all.

                              DTG 150357 Z July,1949.

                    I have asked the CinC that next-of-kin are being assured
of the welfare of all onboard and that they can be informed by Admiralty that
telegraphic facilities are available into "Amethyst" all the time: and also
that they be made aware of CSW system.
You can rest assured therefore that your next-of-kins are being kept fully
"in the picture" of what is going on here as far as it is possible without
giving too much away that can be turned to our disadvantage by the opposition.

You will realise that one of the reasons for the signal which the CinC
sent was to try and let the other side know that we are determined to stand on
our rights. ON this point he made it very clear.

What the next meeting will produce is by no means certain – but at least the
opposition now know exactly how far we are prepared to go here – they will
have to think again.

                              (sd.) J. .Kerans.
                              Lieutenant-Commander ,R.N.
                              16th July,1949.

Distribution ;-   Main NIB. POs.,Stokers,WRIB. (4).

S. 1320E
25M Pads of 200-1-42 (2994)
N.S. 815-9-1320E.

List & S.B. No.	Name	Rating	Port Division and Official No.	Whence Entered	Date	Whither Discharged	Date

Sat. 16th Cont

very good condition. In the evening we had
four large passenger steamer pass the ship,
two up & two down river, one of which
exchanged the courtesy of the sea with us.
Mr Leo still ashore, and no signs of the
stores. The Captain has sent a signal to the
C in C, thanking him for his message to the
whole of us remaining in "Amethyst", a copy
of which is opposite.

Sunday 17th July.

Another hot day seems likely to be ahead of us.
Church on the mess deck at 1105, Lieut (L) Strain
read the lesson. After church all the
ship company were photographed on the quarter
deck in the following groups.
(A) All the thin men led by the Captain.
(B) All the fat men led by the Doctor & of course me.
(C) All the glamour led by Lieut Hett.
(D) All those wearing beards.
(E) Everyone not in any of the above groups.
(F) All the chinese.

This caused a lot of merriment among the
ship and I am perfectly sure that if, Col
Kang or the General had seen us he would
have said, "we shall never make them give in."
And believe me "HE WON'T", our ensign has
been flying since the incident occoured and
although rather tattered and torn now and
riddled with gun fire it is still flying and
will remain so as long as Amethyst stays
afloat.

Mr Leo returned onboard with the stores,
every box having been opened in Ching Kiang.
I had another note from C.P.O. Cunningham. We
got sweets, cigs and nearly everything we asked for,

N.B.
Well
done!
Francis
Quite
right.

L st & S.B. No.	Name	Rating	Port Division and Official No.	Whence Entered	Date	Whither Discharged	Date

List & S.B. No.	Name	Rating	Port Division and Official No.	Whence Entered	Date	Whither Discharged	Date

17<u>th</u> Cont.

including papers & books from the V.J.C. Shanghai, for which we thank them very much indeed, they are most welcome.

During the early part of the afternoon a plane flew over the land and it appeared as if she must have dropped a couple of bombs as clouds of smoke arose as she was flying away.

We had hard luck today everyone was very disappointed, all the week we have been looking forward to the B.B.C's programme listeners choice as they were to broadcast the remainder of our programme today, and we could not receive it, we could hear it very very faint and that was all. Better luck next time we hope?

Monday 18th July.

90 days today and still going strong, I wonder how much longer that B—— is going to keep us? It as been very quiet here today, but very very hot. Mr Leo as gone ashore again with a letter for the Captain. This time he wasn't very long ashore.

Tuesday 19th July.

What a night this as been, not a drop of wind (or should I say "breath") anywhere, the messdecks are like an oven. This evening we set 52 rat traps, but with a nil result. I don't think you can beat the cat for catching them. Today it is red hot again, and how it can get hot. This is by far the worst so far.

Wednesday 20th July.

MIDNIGHT, and cannot get to sleep for the heat, a knock at my door, who can this

L st & S.B. No.	Name	Rating	Port Division and Official No.	Whence Entered	Date	Whither Discharged	Date

List & S.B. No.	Name	Rating	Port Division and Official No.	Whence Entered	Date	Whither Discharged	Date

20TH JULY.

be? I'll bet it is from the Captain.

The messenger enters with a chit from the Captain, O.K. I understand the message.

No more sleep for a while, after (1) one hour no more work either it can wait until the morning, I am wringing wet through with perspiration, so I will go on deck for a breather.

Well its a damn sight worse now, even the vents as pushing hot air around.

I am sure that this is the hottest day yet? Still no news from shore & this is the tenth day since the last meeting. Still they say no news is good news so lets hope that it is right.

21st July '49.

Well, it seems as if we have jumped right into the summer here now, as it keeps getting hotter & hotter each day. And they are finding it hard now down in the engine room, because even on deck in the shade it is up to 102°.

This evening we had a soldier come on-board and apparently he brought a letter from ashore asking the Captain for a meeting. The Captain is leaving the ship shortly after eight a.m.

22nd July '49

The Captain is ashore, he landed with Lt (L) Strain at 0840 and if it took them until half past nine to get to the appointed place, (C.P.L.A Hps) they are having a long meeting as it is now 1530 hours. Still I most sincerely hope that it is not so hot ashore as it is on board here. Things are now beginning to get

L st & S.B. No.	Name	Rating	Port Division and Official No.	Whence Entered	Date	Whither Discharged	Date

List & S.B. No.	Name	Rating	Port Division and Official No.	Whence Entered	Date	Whither Discharged	Date

mighty uncomfortable, and I am afraid that if the oil gets much lower we shall be shutting down again for 48 hours at a time, then it wont be uncomfortable any more, it will be just plain hell. Even to write this I have four sheets of blotting paper under my wrist and it is soaked through now. The Captain returned onboard at about 1600, and brought (4) four bottles of E.W.O Pilsner Beer back with him so we had a raffle in each mess 4 messes for the lucky person was who drank the bottle, it worked out. CH & POs - P.O.S.M. LOGAN. — STOKERS. L.S.M. AUGUSTYNS. — 4 MESS O/SEA HUTCHINSON. 6 MESS O/SEA KEICHER , it does not seem much to get in a raffle, but when you consider that it is 94 days now since we had a bottle, and also that it is about 12/6 per bott it makes you think. We have not heard how the meeting went, but most probably we shall later. Still Col. Kang gave them lunch so it could not have been to bad? Apparently it was not to bad, although our safe conduct down river still hinges on the one thing now and that is Admiral Sir Patrick Brinds signature, they will not accept anyone else, but just as soon as they get that, well then there might be a chance that we shall get our safe conduct.

They are going to try and get us more oil & stores through from Shanghai. ·
I am certain that they will have to do something soon, because it is now beginning to get really grim. —

L st & S.B. No.	Name	Rating	Port Division and Official No.	Whence Entered	Date	Whither Discharged	Date

List & S.B. No.	Name	Rating	Port Division and Official No.	Whence Entered	Date	Whither Discharged	Date

Saturday 23RD July.

We have had rather a humid night, but once again the sun is shining, but I am really pleased to say that there is a wind with it this morning.

Yesterday we had "side screens" fitted along the ships side, but aagain the same as everything else onboard they had to be improvised as the ship side is not even fitted to take the proper martingales and such like, so I should not be suprised, if, when we get a good wind they dont go for a burton? still they are proving very effective as my office is a hell of a lot cooler this morning.

After we shut down last night it was the worst that it as ever been in here, when I came to get my bed I could hardly breathe.

At the present time we are having a lot of trouble with mosquito's, and a kind of moth, which, I should think is only to be found in the Yangtse? because they all seem to collect onboard here, and they are a dammed nuisance. It is a very peculiar sight to see all the arrangements the boys have got to beat these pests. We are also having trouble with the rats, we set about 52 traps for them and they will not walk in, I have heard that they have all got their bags and hammocks packed ready to leave when we do get to Hong Kong.
But the cat as been doing well since we first came up here he as had 12.
The Captain tells me that there will be a possible chance to get a couple of bottles of beer onboard, from Chang Kiang still we must wait & see ⊙

L st & S.B. No.	Name	Rating	Port Division and Official No.	Whence Entered	Date	Whither Discharged	Date

23RD CONT.

The Captain cleared lower decks at 1215 this morning and told us fully about the meeting which took place yesterday. In the first place it was the General who opened the meeting, and the Captain managed to keep him there 50 minutes before he retired from the meeting and left Col Kang to carry on. The General pointed out again that Kang, was his appointed for the talks and also those which are to take place later. He also accused the British of using delaying tactics because the C in C. as not appointed our Captain, Lt Com. Kerans as his official representative by letter and with his personal signature. At this meeting or during the lunch that followed, Kang came right out of his corner and in perfect "English" asked Lt (L) Strain, what the conditions were like for the troops onboard, well after he got over the initial stock he told him good and proper just what it was like. The Col eventually saw a bit of light, and told the Captain that it would be a good thing if Mr Youde could come to help him as an extra interpretor, but will not consider it until he has the C in C's signature, for two hours they were at this one subject hammer and tongs.

There is one good thing, the Captain tells us that he as not seen Kang in this mood before, but puts it down to the fact that the last time they had a meeting he was really rude to Kang, and told him straight that he would refuse to continue these talks any further without Youde.

L st & S.B. No.	Name	Rating	Port Division and Official No.	Whence Entered	Date	Whither Discharged	Date

23rd Cont.

Now all we can do is wait again, and see what happens with the C. in C., if he gets a move on then we should not be here much longer. When I used to play cricket I always used to be very unsteady in the nineties, because when you see the centuary in sight you begin to make false strokes, well we are now in sight of our centuary and I feel entirely the opposite, that is when the fellow on the opposite side is all set for his hundred, just like you want to play that extra little bit harder to get him out. But I really don't think that there is any need to be nervous over this hundred, it is bound to come, the score to date is now 95, but we are still smiling, cheerful and 100% behind the Captain.

Again we have sent a list to TAMAR so that they can send away food parcels to our next of kin, so I hope that they arrive there alright.

Mr Leo as gone home to Nanking for a few days and also to collect 2 million dollars (YEN Min), he took a letter to Jack & Betty for me so I hope that the C.P.L.A. dont search him to much? I am very pleased to say that it as not been so hot today as there as been a nice breeze blowing all the time.

Sunday 24th July.

We have now got a change in the weather again, and today it is really cool with a strong breeze blowing. Church on the mess-deck at 1030 hours. Signals received indicating that the typhoon "Gloria" was is heading our way. All

L st & S.B. No.	Name	Rating	Port Division and Official No.	Whence Entered	Date	Whither Discharged	Date

List & S.B. No.	Name	Rating	Port Division and Official No.	Whence Entered	Date	Whither Discharged	Date

24TH Cont

preparations made to meet this added menace to our
discomfort, all canvas taken down, guns uncovered,
awnings stowed away and now all we can
do is to wait for "Gloria" to embrace us
or pass us by, the later we hope.

Monday 25th July.

Things remained quiet during the night, but the
wind blowing hard and barometer falling.
0730 Wind now gale force and coming in
very strong gusts from N-W. Immediate notice
for slow speed on one boiler and steam on
the capstain, this of course is a purely
cautionary measure as we are still hoping that
it will pass us by. We are certainly feeling
"Gloria" now, blowing & raining like hell and the
Yangtse is really rough. Special sea duty men
warned to remain within easy distance of their
stations. Noon, special sea duty to your stations,
now it is really rough and getting tense.
It is expected that we shall get it passing
us at about 1500, about 14 miles away.
1600, it is now beginning to ease a little.
We dropped the second anchor at about 1210.
This as certainly tested our Port anchor for us,
it as been on the bottom now for over
3 months, and we are very anxious to see
whether it will stand up to the strain?
What will happen if it snaps remains to be
seen, as if we move we are threatened with
destruction, and if it snaps we shall have to
move, so what the hell can we do?
1900, it is at long last showing signs of
breaking, and our cable is holding well.
In the very midst of all the tense-ness of
the last few hours we had the humorous side

L st & S.B. No.	Name	Rating	Port Division and Official No.	Whence Entered	Date	Whither Discharged	Date

25th Cont.

as well, first of all it was a dog sitting on the top of a hay stack floating down river, next it was a chicken on not quite such a large stack. Then we had the highlight a pig swimming down with the tide and the boys of the "Amethyst" trying to lasso him from the ship side, and the pig looking with anxious eyes, as much as to say, for Gods sake do something about it, well we are not repeat not having fresh pork for dinner. A little while later another one came by, but he was further out and we still are not having fresh pork.

Lt (L) Strain our electrical officer, who came on board for a two day trip from Shanghai to Nanking, but who as now done 99 days, was today promoted to Lieutenant-Commander (L), it is also his birthday, & what a birthday, keeping two hour watches on the bridge in howling wind and pouring rain.

Tuesday 26th July.

Everything is back to normal this morning. The C.P.L.A. lost a couple of hay stacks, which were washed away from the river bank which was flooded all the way along. Now we are back again, to the same old game of waiting, waiting and more waiting.

Well yesterday's effort as certainly cost us our oil fuel, and we shall soon have to get some from somewhere, otherwise we shall have to shut right down.

Everyone is now enjoying a little relaxation after the tension of yesterday, and I should say no one ~~desired~~ deserves it more than the captain, who was on the go all the time from morning until evening, and if the cable had parted he would have had to make a quick decision regarding

L st & S.B. No.	Name	Rating	Port Division and Official No.	Whence Entered	Date	Whither Discharged	Date

26th Cont.

the ship and everyone onboard, we are all very much relieved that it was not necessary for him to do so.

The contractor came onboard and brought the beer with him, the first we have had for 99 days, so just to remember this historic occasion I am going to stick the label from my bottle in this book; you see, it is an occasion as this bottle of beer cost 12/6 (twelve shillings & sixpence), rather expensive, but I cannot say that it tasted any better than when we could buy it at 1/3, the only difference of course, being, that we could get what we wanted then, now, we have to take what we can get.

YANGTSE RIVER 啤酒 26/7/49 TRADE

UNION BREWERY LIMITED
UB SHANGHAI

PRICE 12/6 上海 MARK

U.B.PilsenerBeer
Union Brewery Limited
SUCCESSORS TO
Scandinavian Brewery Co., Ltd.
SHANGHAI
12/6 PER BOTTLE

We had a new one today, the side party sampan went on strike, for more rice, from the C.P.L.A. whether they get it or not remains to be seen? what they really want is a kick in the pants. They are getting far to independent. There is an old saying, "Familiarity breeds contempt," and it is certainly true in this case.

M
N
O
P
Q
R
S
T
U
V
W

L st & S.B. No.	Name	Rating	Port Division and Official No.	Whence Entered	Date	Whither Discharged	Date

Wednesday 27th July.

Everything is quiet again today, the wind as gone and now we are settling down to another hot day. 1430 We are now experiencing one of the worst rain storms that we have had yet. 1445, it is all over and beginning to clear up again. Mr Leo should be returning from Nanking today, as he left at 6-30 this morning.

Thursday 28th July.

This is the 100 day of our enforced stay up the Yangtse, and I must say that the conduct of the ships company during this time as been exemplary, it is now anyones guess as to how long we shall remain up here now? still one never knows, it may happen any day, lets hope it is soon, because things are beginning to get really grim now. Mr Leo did not manage to get onboard last night but I expect he will this morning, although, the sampans crew are still on strike.

Yes, Mr Leo did return onboard this morning at about 1015, bringing with him a bag full of "JEN Min" the C.P.L.A. currency, and also a bag of books & papers. One parcel of papers & books & two letters for me from my very good friends Jack & Betty, I really cannot thank them enough, knowing that they are in a worse state than we are, for what they do for me and the remainder of the ships company, no matter if the books & papers are old, it is the thought that goes with them that counts, Thanks, Jack & Betty, one day I hope to be able to repay your kindness in England or should I say Yorkshire?

L st & S.B. No.	Name	Rating	Port Division and Official No.	Whence Entered	Date	Whither Discharged	Date

Friday 29th July.

The sun is shining, the sky clear, the majority of the ships company chipping the rust off the ship and there is some believe me; and, as far as I know the sampan is still in revolt, still one never knows, we shall see what today brings later on. Well the sampan or another one came out to the ship today, one of the old crew had gone over and joined it, but I suppose she had to do so because she has a young baby to keep, still we don't mind who is in it so long as we have one. It is very hot again today. Mr Leo ashore again. Tonight we had a complete black out.

Saturday 30th July.

Well this month has nearly run its course, and we never thought that we were going to be stuck up here all this time, but there it is, we have been, and as far as we can see are just as likely to be here for another month or so. We are of course sincerely hoping that we shall not be. I don't know but I think by all the signs that there must be something brewing. The Captain wants the utmost security onboard, which I have passed around to the CP & PO's. The electricians are to rig red & green lights, and other odds & ends begin to make two & two make five. Little did I know just what was happening or should I say how soon it was happening? The Captain sent for me and told me to have the people on the list he gave me in his cabin at 1940, well we all gathered there, and the words he spoke were these, I have decided to make a break for it to night, and

L st & S.B. No.	Name	Rating	Port Division and Official No.	Whence Entered	Date	Whither Discharged	Date

List & S.B. No.	Name	Rating	Port Division and Official No.	Whence Entered	Date	Whither Discharged	Date

30ᵘᵗ JULY

I dont think there was one of us whose heart did not give an extra beat, I know mine did, not with fear, but I think it must have been with excitement or quiet possibly the feeling that at last we were going to give Kang a smack in the eye. Now I think that this must be what got me all excited, I had about the last signal we received before slipping, from my wife, and she told me that my son was in Portsaid on his way to Hong Kong. never mind Kathleen my darling, I should be home with you shortly, for good, I hope.

Sunday 31ˢᵗ July 1949.

From the time I went into the wheelhouse at about 2130, I do not seem to have a very clear recollection of what took place, lots of orders from the Captain & a hell of a lot of gun fire, we received a hit in the first encounter with the C.P.L.A, but they would have had to blow us right out of the water to stop us, 22 knots was the speed we were making and everything was running fine, more orders more gun fire all the way down, until suddenly, after having just been told to steer as perfect as possible, I got the order "Hard a Star," I had no sooner got this on when I got "Hard a Port," I found out later that we had carved through a junk which got in our way, well the Captain tried to miss it, but these things happen, in any case it was most probably, our lives against theirs, well we won. Later, as dawn was beginning to break, I heard down the voice pipe from the bridge, the most welcome message of all, "The Concord is in sight," so then

L st & S.B. No.	Name	Rating	Port Division and Official No.	Whence Entered	Date	Whither Discharged	Date

31st CONT

we knew that whatever happened passing the forts assistance was there waiting. Well nothing did happen & we had done it. I cannot explain how I felt when the Captain told me that down the voice-pipe, I don't really know whether I wanted to let the tears roll out of my eyes, jump for joy or just fall over, I do know that I felt jubilant.

Eventually I had the order to "ring off main engines"; & I knew them that we had come to anchor & the "Concord" was coming alongside to give us oil, as we only had a very little left. Well we oiled and then found that we were leaving for Hong Kong at 2000 hours.

Monday 1st August 1949.

We are on our way to H.K. alright and expecting to meet the "Jamaica" in the evening. Yes she is here and what a sight she looks, very very welcome to us as we are hoping that she as got mail, she has, and she is steaming around us, the band playing "rolling down the river"; but believe me we didn't do much rolling down, we didn't have time. The mail is onboard, and also Lieut. Berger rejoined us, he had to leave us when we went up river on account of his wounds. Signal from the Flag ship, "Amethyst take guide of Fleet." Well there we are it is all over now except that when we arrive in Hong Kong on the 3rd Aug, there is apparently a hell of a reception waiting for us, and after that I don't think that I shall have time to put any more in this book, so just before I close one of the saddest 3 months

List & S.B. No.	Name	Rating	Port Division and Official No.	Whence Entered	Date	Whither Discharged	Date

I can go home now, my son is
arriving on the "Georgic", as a Royal
Marine to keep the Flag flying.

J. Franks

'Thanks for steering us down so well
The very best of luck'

Michael·E·Fr333ley F/Lt.

List & S.B. No.	Name	Rating	Port Division and Official No.	Whence Entered	Date	Whither Discharged	Date

1ST CONT.

of my Naval Service ending with our triumphant dash, down the Yangtse River, I should like to pay a tribute to the Captain, without whom we should have been lost, his is the brain that thought out all the answers, whilst we were up the Yangtse and the way down, and also most important of all, the brain that brought the "Amethyst" out of hell to "Glory." The ships name & Lieutenant-Commander J.S. Kerans. D.S.O. Royal Navy, will go together into the long history of our Glorious Navy.

In the Captains signal to the C in C. after we got through he said "God save the King" so I will say that I have had the greatest honour that any one could have had, that is to be the Coxswain of "Amethyst" with Lt. Com. Kerans, as my Captain. God Bless you & Yours Sir.

(awarded D.S.O & Promoted to Commander)

I must not forget of course,

Lieutenant-Commander (L) Strain, who as worked like hell all through right to the end, what a two day trip. Thank you Sir.

(later awarded the M.B.E.)

Lieutenant Hett, proved himself a good scout, after all as 1st Lieutenant of any ship he is there to be kicked around. Good Luck to you Sir, someday I hope to be telling my Grand children, "What Admiral Hett, Hi, he was on the Amethyst with me in 1949."

Flight/Lt Fearnley R.A.F. All I can say is "Thanks for coming Sir", may you too, either in the R.A.F or as a Civilian Doctor have all the success you deserve. God Bless.

(awarded the D.S.C).

That all.

L st & S.B. No.	Name	Rating	Port Division and Official No.	Whence Entered	Date	Whither Discharged	Date

List & S.B. No.	Name	Rating	Port Division and Official No.	Whence Entered	Date	Whither Discharged	Date

The Voyage Home.

Singapore.
Penang.
Colombo.
Aden.
Port Said.
Malta.
Gibralta
Plymouth.

What a voyage, everywhere a wonderful reception. Race or creed forgotten, Black, Yellow or White all gave us the same welcome.

This was the finest of them all, homely, spontanious our own people, all united once again. With "Drakes" Drum to welcome us home again.

London.

Rather a strain on every one's nerves, But what an ending after 10,000 miles, to arrive in the Capital of England, to be greeted by "His Majesty The King, Her Majesty The Queen. Princess Elizabeth Princess Margret The Prime Minister and in fact practically every one from the lowest to the highest.

On behalf of myself & my ship company, I would like to say "Thank you one & all" May God Bless you always.

J Frank D.S.M.
Coxswain
H.M.S. Amethyst.
22nd April 1949. to
4th JANUARY 1950.

(awarded D.S.M)

Notes on meeting with Col KANG. C.P.L.A. 5th July 1949

Col Kang. I would like to stress again the points of the meetings held on the 20 & 23rd June 1949. In the last two conversations it has been stated, that if the British side will acknowledge that they INVADED Chinese waters without the authority of the C.P.L.A, an early solution to H.M.S. Amethyst proceeding might be found, and talks continue on the question of guilt and other things after Amethyst as gone.

Col Kang states that the General as recieved a personal message from Admiral Brind, but that the General is not satisfied, as the Admiral did not state that "Amethyst" and the three other British ships were guilty of INVADING Chinese waters.

Col Kang also states that the General always maintains that it was the British warships that caused the incident.

Captain. I am fully prepared to alter the wording to the Generals' requirements.

Col. Kang. Has the C in C. authorised you to alter the words on her behalf? Col Kang would like written authority from Admiral Brind. The General requires that Admiral Brind will authorise Lieut. Com Kerans by written note to the General, that he has been authorised to alter the note.

The Captain then pointed out to the Col (and very much to the point) that Admiral Brind was now in Japan and the chances of getting a letter are very remote. Captain to Mr Leo (our interpertor) and found out that I have been authorised since the 25th June to negotiate, I should NOT be allowed to pass a message if I were not authorised.

Col. Kang indicates that the General requires a note of authorisation from Admiral Brind. The General requires that the Admiral will admit that H.M.S. Amethyst and the three other British warships, INVADED Chinese National waters without the permission of the C.P.L.A. As to the wording of the sentence we can talk about that later on.
At this point Mr Leo was having an argument over the difference in meaning of the words Guilty and Fault. The Captain was very definate (in fact adament) that the word INVADING was NOT going to be used, he told Col Kang that this was an assumption before it has been proved.

The Captain, if you use the word INVASION that means "With intent to INVADE", and it is a very serious word to use. To Mr Leo and point out that the General himself said that this word was NOT to be used.

Col. Kang about the wording of what the General said last time, there might be some difference between the Chinese and English wording. The Col says he is to abide by the Chinese wording, as to the translation of the English into Chinese. He also thinks that it will take some time as this is related to Chinese Sovereignty and has to be as close as possible, IMPUDENTLY (which the Captain wanted to insert instead of INVADED) is a word which modifies the action and the rest is the

Captain 'I assume therefore that he will not accept that word? will he accept
• INDISCREETLY? as that was the very word the General used. Col Kang
says that he wants to express that he means "INVADED CHINESE NATIONAL
RIVER", and that the qualification of the word is most important and
the word itself is of the most importance, but the Admiral or Admiralty
did not mention it. Col. Kang asks that the Admiral recognise that
the Amethyst and the three other British ships involved in the incident
INVADED into Chinese National River and the C.P.L.A frontier without
the permission of the C.P.L.A this being a basic fault on the part
of the British.

Now the Captain really went into action, The word INVADE means to commit
an hostile act or with intent to INVADE which we never intended
to do, as we are neutral. You cannot use as this would mean
that we entered the river Yangste with the intention to INVADE China.

Captain how close in Chinese is the word Guilt to Fault, I don't think he
got an answer to that?

Col Kang wants to impress again does Admiral Brind admit that the British
ships were guilty in entering the River?

Captain I recognize that Amethyst and three other British ships involved in
the incident entered into the Chinese National River and the C.P.L.A
frontier zone, without the permission of the C.P.L.A, this being a
basic fault on the part of the British side, regarding the Yangste incident

Col Kang believes that if we can study this sentence more closely it might help
to bring our views more close together. The reason he has to use the
word INVADING is because Amethyst invaded Chinese Sovereignty and the
Sovereignty is the main consideration.

Now we saw a real diplomat in action and it was good to
listen to! You cannot use that word it means that we are at
war and we are not, we are a friendly nation and always have been.
IF MAO TSE TONG saw that word here, "God help you", In fact I might
just as well ask that wall to speak to me. In fact you mean
C.P.L.A Sovereignty you cannot say China.

Col Kang suggests that we leave this matter to a further meeting?

Captain we shall not stop the conversation just because you want to
you see I want to go on.

. . . .

Col. Kang. I would like to stress again the points of the meetings held on the 20th & 23rd.
June 1949. In the last two conversations it as been stated, that if the British side will
acknowledge that they INVADED Chinese waters without the authorityØ of the C.P.L.A. an
early soluₐtion to H.M.S. AMETHYST proceeding might be found, and talks continue on the
question of the guilt and other things after Amethyst as gone.
Col. Kang states that the General as received a personal message from Admiral Brind, but
but the General is not satisfied, as the Admiral did not state that "Amethyst" and the
three other British ships were guilty of INVADING Chinese waters.
Col. Kang also states that the General always maintains that it was the British warships
that caused the incident.
Captain, I am fully prepared to alter the wording to the General/s requirements.
Col. Kang as the C in C authorised you to alter the words on his behave? Col. Kang would
like written authority from Admiral Brind. The General requires that Admiral Brind will
authorise Lieut. Commander KERANS by written note to the General, that he as been
authorised to alter the note.
The Captain then pointed out to Col. Kang (very much to the point) that Admiral Brind
was now in Japan and the chances of getting a letter are very remote. Captain to Mr. Leo
and point out that I have been authorised since the 25th. June to negotiate, I should NOT.
be allowed to pass a message if I was not authorised.
Col. Kang indicates that the General requires a note of authoriseation from Admiral Brind.
The General requires that the Admiral will admit that Amethyst and the three other British
ships INVADED Chinese National river without the permission of the C.P.L.A. as to the wordi
of the sentence we can talk about it later on. At this point Mr. Leo was having a argument
over the difference of the words Guilty & Fault. The Captain was very definate that the
word Invadingwas not going to be used, he told Col. Kang that this was an assumption before
it has been proved.
The Captain if you use the word invasion that means "With intent to Invade" and it is a
very serious word to use. To Mr Leo and point out that the Gen. himself said that this
word was NOT to be used.
Col. Kang about the wording of what the Gen. ~~says~~ said the last time, there might be some
difference between the Chinese & English wording. The Col. says that he as to abide by the
Chinese wording, as to the translating of English into Chinese. He also thinks that it will
take some time as this is related to Chinese Sovereignty and has to be as close as possible.
impudently (which the Captain wanted to insert instead of Invaded) is a word which modifies
the action, and the ~~word~~ verb is the thing that matters.
Captain I assume therefore that he will not accept that word? will he accept Indiscreetly?
as that was the very word that the Gen. mentioned. Col. Kang says he was to express that
he means"Invaded Chinese National River", and that the qualification of the word is most
important & that the word itself is of the most importance, but the Admiral or Admiralty
did not mention it. Col. Kang asks that the Admiral recognize that the Amethyst and the
three other British ships involved in the incident invaded into Chinese National River
and the C.P.L.A. frontier zone without the permission of the C.P.L.A. this being a basic
fault on the part of the British.
Now the Captain really went into action, . The word INVADE means "To commit an hostile act,
or with intent to invade" which we never intended to do, as we are neutral. You cannot use
the word invade as this would mean that we entered the river Yangtse with the intention
to invade China.

Captain, how close in Chinese is the word Guilt to Fault? I cannot remember if he ever got an answer to that?
Col. Kang wants to impress again does Admiral Brind admit that the British ships were guilty in entering the river?
Captain I recognize that Amethyst and Three other British ships involved in the incident entered into the Chinese National River and the C.P.L.A. frontier zone, without the permission of the C.P.L.A. , this being a basic fault on the part of the British aide, regarding the Yangtse incident.
Col. Kang believes that if we can study this sentence more closely it might help to bring our views more close together. The reason he has to use the word invading is because Amethyst invaded the Chinese Sovereignty and the Sovereignty is the main consideration. Now we saw a real Diplomat in action and was it good to listen to! You cannot use that word it means that we are at war and we are not, we are a friendly nation and always have been. If Mao Tse Tong saw that word here "God Help You". In fact, I might just as well ask that wall to speak to me. In fact you mean C.P.L.A. Sovereignty you CANNOT say China
Col. Kang suggests that we leave this matter to a later meeting?
Captain we shall not stop the conversation just because you want to, you see I want to go on. Then Col. Kang said let us discuss the wording of that word more fully. Col. says that if Admiral Brind can admit ~~that~~ the guilt ~~to~~ of the British on this question. We can discuss the subject of guilt and compensation after the Amethyst as gone. As to the casualities on the British side we cannot accept guilt as these were due to the fault of the British and we cannot express regret. The Captain then pointed out that the Admiral was expressing regret for those suffered by the C.P.L.A. and that he thought that he was being very very fair. Col. Kang the soldiers of the C.P.L.A. who lost their lives died a glorious death in the defence of the Chinese Sovereignty
Col. The Admiral did not mention about the continuation of the discussion or the whereabouts
Capt. pointing to a letter in front of the Col. that statement means that the Admiral is willing to discuss all points after we have gone. The point is that it is going to be settled some time or other, it is going to take a hell of a while but it is going to be settled.
The Col. says that he believes that it is going to be settled but the point must be mentioned
Capt. I presume that the Gen. & Yourself require this matter to be settled quickly?
So I refer to my letter of today asking for Mr. Youde to come from Nanking as an additional interpretor, so that we can get the wording right. He is purely a Chinese and English scholar. About this matter the Col. did not receive the letter and it will have to be discussed with the Gen. Capt. Well he is nearly on his way, and he is coming any hour
Col. How will the exchange of notes take place? Capt. I will sign it.
The Col. as just pointed out that the Admiral should authorise you to sign.
Capt. Once again tell the Col. that the Admiral is in Japan. Col. says try by all means to get a letter in Admiral's writing. But if the Capt. can get a message with his signature using the base of mutual trust we can believe it.
Capt. I want to know why my charts have been kept by the C.P.L.A. Capt? There is not a single defence matter on those charts they are purely navigational charts. How the hell do you think all these other ships go up and down the river? Col. A Chinese pilot as been arranged to take Amethyst down river. Capt I still want those charts and so does a pilot. When I go I shall sail at 0400 C.P.L.A. time 0500 our time. Col. How is the fuel situation? I shall be able to manage, but I still want that from Nanking, and they are having difficulty with your people there. Col. will ring C.P.L.A. Nanking and tell them to hurry. The pilot will be fully

Paid by the A.N.A. Shanghai, and his fare will be paid to return here, and he must come onboard overnight. Are there any other points regarding the journey down that the Col. would like to state?

The Col. thinks that the safe conduct is an easy question.

Capt. How long will it take to inform all concerned?

Col. When we have completed the discussions we shall automaticly arrange the safe journey

Capt. The safe conduct in writing must include in writing that all Batteries and Shanghai have been informed. I shall be flying the flags we are now flying with union flags painted on the top of the guns. Col. It will be in accordance with the International Navigational Code.

Col. Regarding the fuel in Nanking it is up to the company as I have already said that it could be sent. I will try to make them hurry with it.

Capt. Did the dead Chinese Pilots suit cases go to Shanghai? Col. Yes.

Capt. If there is fog on the way down I shall have to anchor until it clears.

Col. If there are any points that we can arrange for you we will do so , we can provide
  every thing you will require.

Capt. I expect to take about ten (10) hours to get down.

Col. How many miles ? 149.

The Col. Wishes you GOOD LUCK on your journey down river.

Col. How many Chinese sailors were killed onboard Amethyst ? Capt told him.

Col. It is hoped that there dependents will get a pension ? This as already been done.

Capt. I shall look for the next meeting on the 8th july, but I am willing to come ashore at any time or in any weather. Ask the Col. To stop the rain.

LIFE ON BOARD H.M.S. AMETHYST

The Admiralty has received the following despatch by radio from H.M.S. AMETHYST. It consists of a general description of conditions on board and of personal messages from the Commanding Officer and from three selected members of the ship's company.

The despatch indicates that all on board are in good heart, that they have plenty of food and plenty of work to do and that, from the Commanding Officer down to the youngest Seaman Boy, all are making the best of their difficult and tedious situation. It is, perhaps, unnecessary to add that everyone on board is anxiously awaiting the day when permission is given for H.M.S. AMETHYST to proceed down river!

The general descriptive message is as follows:-

"The ship is anchored one mile up river from the village of Chon Pi Khen Kou. This village has assumed considerable importance, as it provides our only contact with the shore. Our sampan, which lies alongside all the time, has assumed a like importance, as it is our only means of transport between ship and shore.

"There is a very adequate supply of food on board, most of which comes from New Zealand and Australia and which was in the ship at the time of the action. Our diet is varied by eggs and potatoes from the shore; these are the only local foodstuffs available. The menu is the same for everyone and is arranged by Stores Petty Officer McCarthy of Larne, County Antrim, assisted by Petty Officer Cook Griffiths of Hednesford, near Stafford. No one can complain about the food.

"Our canteen is also very well stocked, which is an invaluable asset. All our 'nutty', the Naval name for chocolate, has gone, but the ice-cream machine is okay. The Canteen is excellently managed by Manager MacNamara of Upper Norwood.

"On board are four officers, sixty-nine British ratings, eight Chinese ratings, a dog and a cat, which somehow survived the action. The latter has caught some rats. Amongst the ship's company are two ratings who have returned to the ship from a hospital at Chingkiang. There are very few amenities, but wireless broadcasts from the B.B.C., Radio Ceylon and Radio Australia are very popular. Our only link with the outside world is by radio and we have only one very overworked operator, Telegraphist French, D.S.M., of Ashburton, Devonshire, who passed this despatch.

"There are only a few films left for the cinema. Physical training gear is used daily to keep people fit. The engine-room and electrical staff have done great work under E.R.A. Williams of Felixstowe (there is no Engineer Officer on board) and Lieutenant Strain of Copnor, the Electrical Officer. They have been responsible for the clearance and repairs to damaged washing facilities, lavatories etc. The ship is now working normal routine and the crew are refitting her themselves. Every Sunday Divine Service is held. Health is good thanks to the doctor, Flight Lieutenant Fearney of the R.A.F. from Blackheath, helped by Stores Assistant Howells of Haverford West, acting as Sick Berth Attendant. Boy Grazier of Leicester City is acting as Hairdresser and also deals with beards, which are becoming most popular. Ordnance Artificer Rees of Rhondda, South Wales, is acting as Schoolmaster and Boys' training continues. All hands are busy working full time and everyone turns a hand to any job that needs to be done. A group photograph of everyone on board has been taken."

The personal messages are as follows:

Lieutenant Commander Simon Kerans, Commanding Officer.

"I pass this personal message to all of you at home, wherever it may be. All on board are in good heart and have shown determination and resource in a difficult situation over a long period. Magnificent teamwork has been evident throughout and no Commanding Officer could ask for better co-operation and assistance. I hope you may receive letters before much longer, but naturally

/I

I cannot give you a better estimate -- negotiations may take time -- but all will be well in the long run.

"To my wife, be cheerful and keep smiling."

Lieutenant Hett of Bawtry, Ardingly, Sussex.

"Lieutenant Strain of Copnor, the Electrical Officer, and myself are the only ship's officers remaining on board from the time of the action. Besides ourselves, there are a Royal Air Force Medical Officer, flown up from Hong Kong, and our Captain, Commander Kerans. For a week we all lived in the radio office, which was the only habitable part of the ship available to officers, as the wardroom, cabins and Commanding Officer's cabin had all been destroyed by gunfire and flooded. We have now been able to clear the Captain's cabin and, after removing the debris and plugged the holes in the bulkheads, have taken up residence there. As First Lieutenant I am assisted by Petty Officer White of London, who is now Chief Bosun's Mate.

"Our first task with the ship's company was to repair as much damage as possible and this was done with very limited resources. Our main job at present is to maintain the machinery in the ship. We have a sampan from a nearby village, operated by three Chinese women, carrying their babies on their backs. This is our only means of contact with the shore, as our own boats have all gone. We pay for this sampan with any food left over on board. I have been ashore in it to arrange meetings for the Captain to negotiate for our fresh food supplies. We barter soap and flour from the ship for eggs and potatoes from the shore, thus varying our diet. Our only means of communication with the river bank is by flags and we therefore have to keep a twenty-four hour look-out on the bridge. There is little variety in our life, but with plenty of work and even more to think about, time goes very quickly and in the evening we sometimes get a game of cards."

Mechanician Holloway of 20 Grove Street, Wellingborough, Northants.

"Except for a natural desire to receive some mail and the slight mental anguish about our present situation and what may lie ahead, life on board is far from empty or unhappy. We are lucky that most of the essential services in the ship are working and that meals are excellent. There is, however, a great shortage of fresh vegetables, but we have been able to get eggs and potatoes from the nearby village, and a great factor has been the adequate stock of rum on board. The weather has been mainly cold and wet.

"We engine-room people have been able to patch up most of the damage in the ship but have been unable to do much about the holes in the outer plating. With plenty of work, we have had little time to sit about and brood and, although we don't expect a safe passage immediately, everybody on board is confident that satisfactory arrangements will be made all in good time."

Ordinary Seaman Mitchell of 20, Fleurs Avenue, Glasgow, S.1.

"In the far distance the first rays of the rising sun silhouette a pagoda which is reflected in the swiftly flowing Yangtze. I close my eyes and listen to the birds, imagining myself at home, but on opening them again and seeing the colourful junks sailing past, I realise where I really am. With my trick on the bridge over, I go below and wonder how to pass the time. Sometimes we play chess, monopoly or darts, but feel a great hankering for beer and suitable blonde barmaids to serve it. You at home have all the excitement of Derby Day, but our only excitements are marbles or ludo on the mess-decks!"

4th November 1949.

Sir,

    I am commanded by My Lords Commissioners of the Admiralty to inform you that they have learned with great pleasure that, on the advice of the First Lord, the King has been graciously pleased to award you the Distinguished Service Medal for outstanding courage, skill and devotion to duty in H.M.S. AMETHYST when she was fired upon by Chinese military forces while she was proceeding to Nanking on 20th April 1949, and subsequently when forced to remain for three months in the Yangtze River under the constant watch of shore batteries until she made her daring escape down the River on the night of 30th/31st July 1949.

    This Award was published in the London Gazette of 1st November 1949.

        I am, Sir,

          Your obedient Servant,

Acting Petty Officer (Q.M.1) Leslie Frank, D.S.M.

3816.—Honours and Awards—" London Gazette " of 1st November, 1949
(H. & A. 349/49.—11 Nov. 1949.)

ADMIRALTY,

Whitehall, S.W.1.

1st November, 1949.

The KING has been graciously pleased to give orders for the following appointment to the Distinguished Service Order and to approve the following awards :—

For outstanding courage and devotion to duty in H.M.S. " Amethyst " when she was fired upon by Chinese military forces while she was proceeding to Nanking on 20th April, 1949, and subsequently when forced to remain for three months in the Yangtze River under the constant watch of shore batteries until she made her daring escape down the River on the night of 30th/31st July, 1949 :—

Distinguished Service Cross

Lieutenant Peter Egerton Capel Berger, R.N.

Distinguished Service Medal

Acting Petty Officer (Q.M.1) Leslie Frank, D/JX.667520.
Engine Room Artificer Second Class Leonard Walter Williams, D/MX.55557.

Posthumous Mention in Despatches

Surgeon Lieutenant John Michael Alderton, M.B., B.S., R.N.
Ordinary Seaman Reginald Jack Wright, D/SSX.831955.

Mention in Despatches

Lieutenant Keith Stewart Hett, R.N.
Electrical Artificer Third Class Lionel Harry Chare, D/MX.55237.
Petty Officer (C.1) William Henry Freeman, D/JX.149820.
Boy First Class Keith Cantrill Martin, D/JX.836190.
Stores Petty Officer John Justin McCarthy, D/MX.57988.

(Other awards to H.M.S. " Amethyst " were published in the *London Gazette* No. 38604 of 6th May, 1949, and No. 38683 of 5th August, 1949.)

For great courage when he was flown to H.M.S. " Amethyst " on 21st April, 1949, and joined her under heavy fire. With great skill and untiring devotion to duty he rendered invaluable services to H.M.S. " Amethyst's " wounded.

Distinguished Service Cross

Flight Lieutenant Michael Edward Fearnley, 59425, R.A.F.

For outstanding courage and devotion to duty while serving in H.M. Ships " London ", " Consort ", and " Black Swan ", during their attempts to assist H.M.S. " Amethyst " while under very heavy gunfire on 20th/21st April, 1949 :—

Bar to the Distinguished Service Order

Captain Peter Grenville Lyon Cazalet, D.S.O., D.S.C., R.N., H.M.S. " London ".

To be a Companion of the Distinguished Service Order

Commander Ian Greig Robertson, D.S.C., R.N., H.M.S. " Consort ".

Listinguished Service Cross]

Mr. Reginald Smith, Senior Commissioned Gunner, R.N., H.M.S. " London ".

Distinguished Service Medal

Able Seaman Alan Earle Dudley, D/JX.315663, H.M.S. " London ".
Bandmaster Frederick George Harwood, R.M.B.X. 368, R.M., H.M.S. " London ".
Leading Stoker Mechanic Tony Arthur Oliver Johnson, D/KX.98914, H.M.S. " Consort ".
Chief Petty Officer Henry William Robinson, G.M., D/JX.133428, H.M.S. " Consort ".

Posthumous Mention in Despatches

Chief Writer Patrick Joseph Stowers, P/MX.59958, H.M.S. " London ".

15th November 1949

Dear Mr. Frank,

      I am writing to confirm the
arrangement made with you on my behalf
by the Secretary of the R.N. & R.M. Association
that you should call at my Parlour here at 11
a.m. on Monday next, the 21st instant, when
the Sheriff and I will have the pleasure of
offering you Civic greetings.

      I extend to you a cordial
invitation to bring your wife and mother
(or other close relative) with you.

      Yours sincerely,

Lord Mayor.

P.O. Frank,
c/o 114, Anlaby Park Road South,
Kingston upon Hull.

Royal Naval Hospital,
Stonehouse,
Plymouth.

18th December 1949,

MEMORANDUM.

YANGTSE INCIDENT
22ND APRIL - 3RD AUGUST 1949.

This memorandum is addressed to all officers, chief petty officers, petty officers and men who served under my command in H.M.S. Amethyst during her long period of internment and subsequent escape from Communist forces in the Yangtse river.

2.   As the year of 1949 draws to its inevitable close, it is fitting to place on record a few important points which emerge after all these months, which have made 1949 a year that none of us will ever forget.

3.   Incidents of this nature in peace are extremely rare, and "Amethyst's" stay in the Yangtse Kiang has no parallel in history. The fact that everyone from the oldest to the youngest faced the situation with poise and equanimity was indeed salutary, and my greatest asset. The spirit of leadership and devotion to duty was fully exemplified by officers and senior ratings; this after all is the fundamental basis of our training and the essence of everything that the Royal Navy has stood for in the past and stands for in the present and the future.

4.   One and all, you have shown that courage and fearlessness in adversity are still the finest attributes of the British peoples. And, finally, team-work and co-operation were predominant from the start to the finish, without this "bond of fellowship", all might well have been lost; that no link in the "chain" was broken was a first class effort. To the younger ratings I say, bear this in mind - you have a future ahead - the basis of any trade is sound discipline and commonsense in an emergency.

5.   Most of us are now separated, and will go our devious ways, whether in civilian life or in the Service. I wish you all the best of luck in the future; it has been a pleasure to serve with you all.

6.   Please take this memorandum as my final words to you - I am sick and in hospital for some time, and this is the only means I can convey what I wish to impart.

7.   And in conclusion I quote the final paragraph of my covering letter to the Yangtse Incident report:-
        "Our prayers were answered, and escape was achieved without loss of life and serious damage. FAITH is not the least of the lessons to be learnt when in adversity".
        Let us not forget this very true statement.

Lieutenant Commander
Royal Navy.

Distribution:-
Lieutenant Commander (L)G.B. Strain, R.N.   Commanding officer,
Lieutenant K.S. Hett, R.N.   H.M.S. Amethyst.
Flight Lieutenant M.E. Fearnley, R.A.F.   3rd Frigate Flotilla.
All Chief Petty Officers,   Far East Station.
Petty Officers and ratings who served
in the Yangtse river on board H.M.S. Amethyst from 22nd April 1949, to
arrival at Hong Kong on 3rd August 1949.